Mania, Mania, Mania

The step-by-step approach to Hypermania, Hypomania & Bi-polar

"One million people commit suicide every year"
World Health Organisation

Mania, Mania, Mania

All rights reserved, no part of this publication may be reproduced by any means, electronic, mechanical, or photocopying. No documentary, film or in any other format without prior written permission of the publisher.

Published by
Chipmunka Publishing Ltd
PO Box 6275
Brentwood
Essex CM13 1ZT
United Kingdom

Copyright © 2008

Cover Image by Marie Berger

A record of this book is in the British Library

Mania, Mania, Mania

About this Book

An international bestseller, this book is broken down into bite-sized chunks. It was first published in 2005 by Chipmunka Publishing, and the author was Sushi I toy (an anagram of IS THIS YOU).

The ideal is to challenge the reader into an psychoanalyze   each section.

These sections are called *Think about it.*

This is a step-by-step approach to Hypermania, Hypomania & Bi-polar

The challenge to the reader is to apply grey matter.

Mania, Mania, Mania

Mania, Mania, Mania

Mania affects many people in many ways:

1in 4 people will have mania in their lives
1 in 3 women who give birth will suffer baby blues
1 in 3 appointments with doctors concern mental health
1in 2 cases of baby blues will affect the other partner
2:1 of mania suffers affect two or more other people (family, work mate or others)

<u>Think about it.</u>
YOU ARE AFFECTED, DIRECTLY OR INDIRECTLY

Mania, Mania, Mania

Mania, Mania, Mania

Foreword

Have you ever wondered what drives Richard Branson? Why Ryanair is growing? Or why Easyjet has so many sister companies?

Or how high-powered people think they can get away with it with companies the like of Enron, Tyco and others, above reproach and untouchable?

This book gives insight into the types of people that make it work. Some are in-your-face and some are behind the scenes. By the end of the book you will be able to spot these people, think like them when you have to and be the real you.
Anyone who slows them down "does not get it".

Mania gives you edge over the competition, mere mortals just crumble. But like a gun in untrained hands, you can leave disaster in your wake.

There are four sections within the book. Hyper mania described covers the medical aspects of the condition. Hyper mania in personal life, once you understand the person we can then talk about the condition, covers the 24/7 of a hyper maniac, you will see that his home life is often different and understand why. This covers a real hyper maniac that lives the trails, highs and lows. Hyper mania in business covers the working and pure moneymaking machine of a hyper maniac. You could increase your income or life style by following

Mania, Mania, Mania

these rules. I am a hyper maniac what now? Covers the next step.

You have to start somewhere, expect the unexpected.

You get it or you do not. Heaven can't help you if you do not get it!!!

You can learn to control it.

Think about it.

Without the high of being in business or the knife-edge between greatness and sanity, very few of the great things would have been achieved.

There are to extremes of mania, however there is also the grey section in between, people can move fluidly between the poles of mania. There are often direct triggers for this condition to happen.

Mania does give extreme power to the person, however how this power is focused, IS always the issue.

Mania, Mania, Mania

With uncontrolled mania, you are the unexpected, with controlled mania YOU control the situation, not it controls you.

Control of mania, whether personal or for others is the key. YOU need to learn how to do this.

<u>*I think therefore I am - read this book and you are!!*</u>

Mania, Mania, Mania

Dedication

To all those that understand I give you power, to those who do not, you still don't get it.

To my parents, my environment and contacts, you made me what I am today.

You have to learn otherwise you will fall foul of these people.

Think about it.
You are a by-product of your environment. If you want to improve, change the environment or it will consume you.

There is a thin line between temper and mania.

Mania, Mania, Mania

Mania, Mania, Mania

Book One Mania described

What is the purpose of this book?

Everything has a purpose, and this book sets out to challenge **YOU,** the reader.

Think about it.
This book is to challenge YOU, not a work of fiction that you can put down not to affect your life again. Just like LIFE itself it's a challenge.

People with MANIA: hypermania or hypomania are more likely to do what they have to do, rather than what they want to do.

Think about it.
People with Mania are compelled to do things. For both good and bad, for them or for others.

Until it finally sinks in, you will usually find your failure is based on your hard-headed experience. You succeed in business because you failed five times before.

You have to learn, and here you will.

Mania, Mania, Mania

Think about it.
The most informed education is self- taught. However this is the most painful.
Second-hand experiences are OK, but not as effective as why you do not eat or drink things.

Success and failure are also best learnt first hand.

This book is intended to reveal the inner thoughts of hyper mania and hypomania, you will either be interested or not.

For those who want to develop themselves or **understand for** others it will be an interesting read. For those that can't understand, go and buy Harry Potter. Because people that don't get it slow hyper maniacs and hypomaniacs down.

You can do so much more and if you want to, this is the book. If not, carry on with your life and expect no more that you get. Do you want to start understanding yourself?

You will reap what you sow, <u>challenge everything</u>. **Expect nothing**.

Mania, Mania, Mania

The world is changing, you need to evolve or die out. This book is intended to help you start to evolve. But for you to evolve, you must start to understand.

People with hyper mania or hypo mania are more likely to do what they have to do, rather than what they want to do.

Until it finally sinks in, you will usually find your failure is based on your hardheaded desire.

You might get an underlying trend of NLP (Neuro-Linguistic Programming). It's what a good maniac uses.

Ever questioned why you do what you want to rather than what you have to?

Ever wanted to do more?

It is here and more…………..

Think about it.
This book is not intended for drones, the readership is looking for something else. It might be control of their lives or environment.

Mania, Mania, Mania

You will not get it first time. Few do. You need to really think about it.
Hence this book is now in a bite- sized format.

Question both yourself and your environment. THEN DO SOMETHING ABOUT IT.

NLP does this, but not on its own, it needs YOU.

*The only thing holding YOU BACK IS **YOU.***

Mania, Mania, Mania

Two Types of Mania

Hypermania and Hypomania

The dictionary describes hypermania as excessive enthusiasm (inward) while hypomaniac is expressed in a more outward way (in-your-face).

A medical professional would describe it as a state of mind characterised by excessive cheerfulness and increased activity.

I would just say it's a rollercoaster.

Think about it.
You can be either, at times you could move from one to the other. The traits of either make you mostly one or the other. It is possible to move from one to the other over a period of time.

Mania, Mania, Mania

Hypermania

My thanks to John D Gartner and his book, *The Hypo Manic Edge*, ISBN 0743243447. It helped establish the two extremes, both of which I have suffered.

This book helped me define the divide between hypo maniac and a hyper maniac.

The biggest similarity is that they are **not afraid of death.**

Conversely, the dreams are a theme to the maniac. While often dreams are forgotten within 10 minutes of waking the maniac can remember more dreams. The hyper will have dreams of power while the hypo will have dreams of doing. Some of these dreams might not come true for 10 years. Just like déjà-vus.

Hypomania and hypermania are mild forms of mania, the hypomaniac being full of drive, confidence and great plans, while the hypermaniacs think in logical patterns. They know where they have to go, and get there in baby steps.

This is not a condition you could be locked up for. There is no medication for it, while being similar is not the same as being Bi Polar.

Mania, Mania, Mania

Hypo: the charismatic leader
Hyper: behind that leader

Hypos talk fast, think fast and act fast.
Hyper, talk slow (do you get it?), think fast and act according to demands.

Bi polar and maniacs can reach denial, this is key as this often acts as a way for them to overcome the obstacle.

Both hide pain, although this is more visible in hypomaniacs as they are in the limelight.

Both know good ideas when they see one, hypers and hypos are not exclusive, you can progress between them, often a progression from hypo to hyper is normal.

Think about it.
These are very hard to spot, because they blend in (see later) However, logical thinking often gives them away. Often they can rely on logic not "gut". There are no real tests, other than logic itself. Apart from the limelight or confrontation (they do not like too much of either).

Mania, Mania, Mania

Hypomania

Hypos are self-centred - me, me, me. Hypo maniacs think big, create the dots and then someone else has to join them.

Often found playing around with the opposite sex, they have a very high sex drive. They live life in the fast lane.

Think about it.

Because these are easier to spot, you know about them. However DO NOT confuse them with Bi-Polar type 2.
The easiest way to tell is by behaviour traits, they like spending other people's money and not their own, while Bi-Polars spend both.

Mania, Mania, Mania

Can You tell the Difference?

Hypers are sure of their direction and get there by baby steps. They consider their close contacts (or other people) and might even make a detour, to help someone they trust.

The Hypers will undermine by quoting facts, which are the key defence and act like mud (slowing down) because the opposition will not expect it (normally Hypos). They will then talk to each advisor to win them over, rather than a frontal assault on a group.

The standard response is to move faster, get aggressive, pile on the energy: a frontal assault on the apposing force.

Hypers created A) and B), then race there. However it's a one-horse race: them.

They are found in very safe relationships, stable environments with stable family life. They tend to look after others more.

However they are still a **coiled spring**. Although I am not a doctor, I understand the medical view of hypo mania, and I am a hyper maniac myself. This book confirms what I have known for over 20 years. There are still few people

Mania, Mania, Mania

who understand either. Either inside or outside the medical profession.

These people are focused to learn and react - if they do not know the subject this time, they will next time. Just watch out, they may use disinformation, divide and conquer or something equally nasty.

They do have NLP built in; with most people it's an optional extra. Or some do not use it at all.

Eye contact is treated differently; one will stare until you submit, the other will use it only when they need to.

They come in two flavours, in-your-face and stealth. Watch out for the stealth ones as they are really special and in control.
Ask yourself these questions:

1. if someone is in your way, will you knock them over?
2. are you the life and soul of the party?
3. do you need less than 6 hours sleep?

Think about it.
These types are different, both to the extreme, however you need to be able to identify both.

Mania, Mania, Mania

Hypo maniac-In-your-face

They will invade your personal space and sit eyeball to eyeball in front of you until you submit. They are very good at negotiation and discussion; their fast reflexes enable them to process data quicker (they do have extra high IQ and even more cunningly emotional intelligence).

On the phone you have to say yes, because they force you to do so. This is similar to people with other medical conditions like Asperger syndrome. However these are the sharpest of the bunch. Sure they have their down days, but these are hard for the average person too.

They have a lower amount of planning due to the pressure that they put on people. However this is how they get things done, they see the higher level.

Most have inbuilt desire to share information (unlike the stealth), they have high trust and at times can resort to physical violence or outbursts.

They are the people you can see, they are in-your-face until you submit.

This type of hyper maniac often creates the environment and atmosphere, more often as tension, discussed later.

Mania, Mania, Mania

Think about it.
You know when you have been "done". These people force the issues.

Confront them with facts, this is one of the only powers you might have. Free will is not enough, even setting traps might not help you. Hypos bounce from one job to the next, and feed off uncertainty.

Mania, Mania, Mania

Hypermania - Stealth

Ask yourself these questions:
- if someone is in your way, will you have a planned way round them?
- in a party are you looking at other people's interaction?
- do you need less than 6 hours sleep?
- do you use sleep to plan?

No need to lock up your daughter (that's in your face, who would like her) , but your mouth (the information you put out will be used against you)

A different animal but the same family. They take in the data and feed it back in such a way that you have to follow them.

These are the quiet ones, always thinking and planning, they pounce like a coiled spring.

They are often found beside the hypomaniac (or both at the same time). You have to know what to look out for as they are hard to spot. They are so cunning, but they do pay attention to details and join up the dots.

They get to know their contacts' patterns, down to eating and drinking times. They can sense the tension on a phone call. Within companies, expect

Mania, Mania, Mania

them to know the inner movements within a short period of time. Even in conversations they can read body language and move the conversation without need to know the local tongue.

They are very trustworthy - they have high respect and HATE fools. They tend to keep their own council and blend in. Boys blend in and plan because they know that planning and preparation is everything. They are results-driven, but they target their results, to the outcome they want.

This it the enemy you can't see until it's too late. They are the people you can't see coming. While the in-your-face you can see a mile off, this type might be right next to you. In military campaigns they are best described as sleepers.

It is best to have them on your team, they need to have faith in you.

You will not see these people, they do not stick out and they are often found behind someone.

They could be a good **FD** (Finance Director) , hiding behind a **CEO.** They gather information on so many different levels. The only clue to find one might be that most people consider these people as sad cases. They understand and can apply Six Sigma, TQM, and Fiscal 2, along with other work practices discussed later in the book. They are good at reasoning on many levels and talking to all

Mania, Mania, Mania

classes at their own level. They are not the life and soul of the party, but people look up to them.

They use disinformation, just like the prisoner in the 1960's cult TV programme. They might learn a subject for later, and I mean ten years later. They can spot future trends and add to their skillset at any time.

This type feeds off the environment and atmosphere, often uses Jedi powers to sense the forthcoming debate or mood swings as discussed later. They appear more laidback, because they lull you into a false sense of security. Some call this perception, but the reality is that you open up more and this gives them more data to use against you.

They both know what they want and how they are going to get there. It's the same journey, however by different directions. There is so little evidence of fear that they resemble a bull elephant.

Do not try and use or abuse these people, you will be the victim

Think about it.
These are calm collective types, they are non-confrontational. Think of them if you will as "the men in Black". They blend in and no one remembers them.

Mania, Mania, Mania

They either have NLP or MBTI built in.

They enjoy programs like CSI (Crime Scene Investigation), depending on how good they are they can even tell you the plot, and who did it.

Others see them as a sniper, single and focused.

Mania, Mania, Mania

Bi polar

The dictionary describes bi polar as two extremes.

A medical professional would describe it as an euphoric mood that changes rapidly to irritability where thought and speech are rapid to the point of incoherence and connections between ideas may be hard to follow. Treatment is usually done with drugs such as lithium or phenothiazines. They suffer episodes of depression and mania.

Bi polar type one: classically depressed

Bi polar type two: mood swings, highs and lows

I would just say it's a **trainee** hyper maniac and very bright.

I know a number of bi-polars and they are great people, but they are very much in-your-face. They demand a great deal in time and effort. I would rather be with a group of people with bi-polar syndrome than most other groups.

They are very bright. Anyone who has read ***A Can of Madness*** by Jason Pegler will see what the life of a bi-polar can do.

Mania, Mania, Mania

Some people I know have this condition but are unable to control it (more later in the book.)

The bi polar person has high and low days. They are often given medication to control the mood swings. However a simple monitor of food and drink intake takes the lows out.

Their thirst for knowledge is vast, they will read and do anything. I do mean anything.

They are very good salesmen, similar to the in-your-face hyper mania people.

Bi polar people have what is known as mania. When they are stable ask them what to do so you can help them when they are down.

This is a proven medical condition, **unlike** hyper mania and hypo mania.

Think about it.
One trait that you might notice is excessive spending. One woman met a man (20 years her junior) and spent £1,600 on a car for him, along with treats everyday. Even though she was married to a loving husband, she amassed debts to the tune of £20,000. To hide these bills from everyone including herself, she placed the envelopes in a special drawer. It was not until she

Mania, Mania, Mania

could not spend any more that she admitted her wrongdoings.

Mania, Mania, Mania

Physical and Mental health

Both the physical and mental are so related it's hard to keep them apart. The more of the right food you eat the better your body is. You can't do a full presentation after a heavy night on the beer.

Mental health is going to be the second highest global killer from 2020 according to the World Health Organisation.

The number of external factors that influence mental health are increasing. As the McDonald's generation, PlayStation generation and pill popping generation take over the world becomes a harder place to live in. This creates social disorder, as they can't communicate and find physical activities hard to do.

A simple example is stress, let's say that you have children and they play up. How do you deal with that stress? Kick the cat? Red wine? Weed? Walk in the garden? Hit them?

But if this stress goes on too long the impact is going to change you.

Think about it.
Mind body and spirit is the key. Too much stress or high life does kill. Do most things in moderation, but do not be boring.

Mania, Mania, Mania

On many levels you need to be able to communicate with your environment and it needs to communicate with you.

Likewise with your body, if your body is telling you it needs sleep, do not wait for death to set in. Give it some sleep

You are what you eat.

It's true: you are conditioning your body, therefore that thing they call a balanced diet is critical to keeping your body in trim. Both mind and body depend on what goes into your mouth. Therefore as discussed later, a poor diet can lead to lack of energy. The mind will start slipping and it could cost you your job or even your life.

They say two can live as cheap as one, however this is not about food but rather mental stimulation.

There is a delicate balance in all you eat or drink - too much coconut milk can produce the runs. While not enough vitamin C, produces sore gums, teeth and lips. To be at your peak you need a balanced diet.

The caffeine-based drinks popular with young people are very scary. In clubs there is low alcohol

Mania, Mania, Mania

consumption and increased sales of caffeine products lead to greater highs. However this is at a cost to the person. How do you take someone down who has had too much caffeine? Hospitals near the big nightclubs in Spain are finding out.

The new replacement to E is Special K. This puts people in a trance and gives a different kick. However it tends to kill more brain cells than E or cannabis.

Too much or too little sugar can kill. There have been many cases of people being hypoglycaemic all over the world. This creates all sorts of stress in the body which, in some cases, leads to the body burning out.

Your body has natural chemicals, like lithium, iron, water etc without these you would soon die.
Look after your body - you only get one.

Think about it.
Mind, body and soul need to be in a good state. Too many drugs and even your body might give up on YOU!!!

Drugs include class A-C, but also include too much coffee or tea. Those drinks after work or at home are a killer too.

Mania, Mania, Mania

Your body needs the right balance, of everything.

Chipmunka do an amazing video of how schizophrenics handle their condition by drumming or meditation. You can control your body without external drugs by a system called NLP.

If you have seen *Super Size Me*, the food was (in large amounts) very harmful. We live in an age where we spend less time eating. Food preparation is a chore and washing up not on the agenda.

Look at the developed world where eating is part of the culture. For example, in Italy a meal can take 3 hours. Better than 2-4 minutes that the fast food chains allow.

However 50 years ago, families sat down at a table. Yes, table, the thing that you sit at in PROPER food restaurants. Where there was no TV, there was interaction and conversation. Now you will eat, in front of the TV, something that's been prepared en masse and blasted in the microwave. TV dinners have been designed by the TV companies to keep you there in front of the TV.

Go on a holiday, on a desert island and you will eat freshly prepared food without additives. You will focus on life and not the TV. Your mood set will also change and with no external demands you will destress and feel happy.

Mania, Mania, Mania

Think about it.
Food is the visible sign of how good you are. Eating fast or fatty food will show that you really do need help. While eating fresh food will be helping your body.

Your weight is affected by what you are eating, with extra weight comes those hard to make disappear issues of, being out of breath or having diabetes. In some countries overweight (or Clinically Obese) people are refused medical treatment, or have to buy two airline seats.

Stress junkies are to be avoided at all costs. They feed on stress and give it to others.

The Times newspaper in the UK reported that Britain counts £100Bn as for the cost of stress in the workplace (May 16 2005). The article goes on to explain that the poor relationships, including low levels of trust, lack of supportiveness and no one that listens, along with long shifts, bad travel conditions and work overload or under load all build up to produce stress.

The facts and figures have been supplied by a Mind report. This is the tip of the iceberg; the balance is as always delicate. This is why the report refers to work overload and work under load.

Mania, Mania, Mania

Work overload is easy to explain, however under load is best explained as "I am Bored".

There will always be those people taking a sick day or bunking off but here will be hard workers too. In Japan you have no power, but if you are not at your desk for 8 hours a day you are told off.

The UK has become a 24/7 way of living. You can shop at a supermarket from 8am Monday to 10pm Saturday. I like shopping between midnight and 6am, the shop is empty of people and they have real staff during these hours.

Anyone who has watched Sky programmes like "Paul McKenna's I can change your life" will see that the process deals with the psychical and the mental. They are both interlinked in such a way and dealing with one can create an imbalance.

Have you got it? Hypermanics or bi-polar types are dangerous, while hypomanics are the one to watch.

Think about it.
Some stress keeps you going. Too much and you will burn up.

The mind does control the body, however YOU can control both.

Mania, Mania, Mania

There are three types of people you are going to meet in your life watch out for all of them.

Bi-polars (type 1 and 2) will be on the increase as Bi-polar triggers increase in everyday life. Furthermore, expect mania to be commonplace, but used as the excuse not the reason.

Mania, Mania, Mania

Perception & reality

Perception is described as process for each of the senses by identifying the environmental stimuli, sensory receptors and path of sensation.

Reality is more tactile (but only just.)

The Magic Circle use deception and it is only when you see how the trick is done that it becomes reality.

Think about it.
The in-your-face will use fast cars and flash watches (power dressing) to win you over. The stealth will be clean-shaven, wearing a normal suit, but the mind will be their weapon.

In a more down to earth example the perception can be described as: there are two men, one with a Rolex watch, an Audi TT and a four bedroom house, long drive and pool. One with no watch, a ten-year-old car and a four-bedroom house.

Reality is painful.

Think about it.
Social conditioning is similar to perception: you see a policeman, you see authority.

Mania, Mania, Mania

However if you do not understand who the uniform this can often be used against you.

Next time you get a call from someone saying they are a supplier but just need to check bank details or date of birth just say give me a contact number and I will call you.

The same is true if a uniformed person comes to your door, have they been requested to come or is the ID fake?

Does one person have more debts than assets, and someone else owe no one anything. Or the other way round? Which one is happier with his lot?

You might meet someone and think that they have it all but really they owe it all and are unhappy to boot.

It's the hyper maniac that has everything; he knows when to change his car, while the hypo maniac has outgoings in excess of incomings.

A hyper maniac uses both, but does make sure that they are correctly used. Like a good salesman you might talk about your investments into companies but not boast. Net worth is a difficult subject. Hyper maniacs and bi polar are not normally liars, they

Mania, Mania, Mania

might bend the truth but they know that they can be found out.

They are into the area of perception. You talk to an in-your-face person and they make you think that you are the centre of their universe. What is said is not as important as what was implied.

For example: on a recent trip away, the perception was not far from reality. Some wanted to believe the trip was for business and others knew it was a birthday gift. While the reality is it was both for business and pleasure.

The hyper maniac uses both of these, however they use different measure of in-your-face (more reality), because they want physical things. The stealth is about perception.

An example is in one job I had some years ago, I liked the company car and had the option of buying it. I also had another job lined up. I need to move fast. I ended up buying the car for £3500 undervalued and still leaving the employer without a clue. How? Well, I followed the law change that I had the option of a car, I found out what the company book value was and the real value. I (without being in-your-face) showed the car to be the wrong car for the company, as well as me as I paid too much tax. I then convinced the company that I needed the money rather than the car and I purchased the car. Three years later I sold the car

Mania, Mania, Mania

to my brother in law for the same some of money (also using stealth).

Hyper maniacs are 5th dan in the arts of perception and reality. They can do what real black belts do and use the enemies' weapons against them.

How? Well they carry on testing you.

If you say that you are a director of a company, they, hyper maniacs, do a company search, visit you or phone you up. Then if you commit to doing something, this will be followed up. Their personal database on you will be extensive, contained in grey matter.

Why do hyper maniacs push you? To undermine you and get you to submit. They will present a good story, but like the good magic man (covered later in this book) and you will be forced to look at the right hand not the left. The facts will be facts but in such a way you will be forced to admit that they did not lie. Hyper maniacs tend not to lie, they might bend the truth but they do not lie. You might be forced to lie to save yourself from commitment. Don't forget your lies come back to haunt you.

This is why they make great sales people. Use the in-your-face chap to open the door and use the Stealth to develop that relationship. The customer will go nowhere because your team would know more about the business than the clients' staff themselves.

Mania, Mania, Mania

A real example:

I was involved with a company in the North East. It was a family-run company with a turnover of £35m. They sold out to London-based investors and appointed a CEO. While I have only been to the company four times before change of ownership I had gathered much data. During the presentation of supply solutions to the CEO, his PA interrupted the meeting asking for an aerial shot of the building. He was new and the handover so quick he really did not know where any of the company files were. My reply was simple that if he could not find a copy I could supply him an image from the very laptop I was presenting from. My colleague and I had a laugh about this shortly after as whenever he required further information we received a call. His role of CEO was undermined. We know he was on thin ice because he did not understand the company or how it worked. He did not deserve the high salary he was being paid.

Think about it.
You can recall you own examples, you need to be able to assimilate this information, why the example was used, was it good or bad.

You learn by first- hand experiences, however if you do not reflect on them, how can you learn?

Mania, Mania, Mania

Take time out NOW to write down and reflect on the times you have been used and times you have used others, both to good and bad.

By doing this you will be far more focused and won't drift through life like a drone.

Focus, and do not lose focus.

Mania, Mania, Mania

Starting with you (the power of one)

You may have seen films like *Cry Freedom*. Anyone knowing an oppressed culture or people will understand that the vision started with one person. Martin Luther King led the black people to freedom. Could this have happened with a white middle class person? I think it unlikely.

Ghandi and Genghis Khan travelled in their countries, uniting them to fight the oppressor or acting as the oppressor. They started with one person, one vision.

Think about it.
A single person does have the power, there are examples of this everyday. You do have to be focused and passionate about your subject, this can win the day.

However it might take months, years or a lifetime to achieve the aims. In more hostile cases it can cost a life too.

A very English example is that of Prince Charles. For decades he has been labelled (incorrectly) as a loony that talks to plants and rambles on. HOWEVER after 30 years,

Mania, Mania, Mania

his comments about the environment are the same tune as everyone else's. He wrote it, and sang it first.

Innovation and creation (thinking outside the box) are often seen, as the ramblings of a mad man.

Yes, the earth is round!!

You can reprogram yourself into a better person; I would recommend *Teach Yourself NLP* by Steve Bavister and Amanda Vickers (Hodder Headline, ISBN 0340 812575).

You hold the key to turn your life around. A person with a drink problem can do nothing unless he understands and admits he has a drink problem.

A nice way that a drunk woman explains the problem is that others only have a drink problem if they drink more than me and I do not like them. They are a drunkard and they see a small aspect of someone's life that is wrong, while theirs is just as damaged.

Think about it.
You can do it - the only thing holding you back is YOU.

Mania, Mania, Mania

Did Ghandi have superhuman powers? No, he was clever, smart and in touch with the people.

What do you want to do with your life? This is an underrated question.

I have seen people walk on fire; I have seen minds changed forever. The power of the mind is very powerful. However historically it has sometimes been used for good, often for bad. Some are weak and some are strong, they often do it for different reasons, normally fear or greed.

By being positive often tips the balance. You will see a number of books on being positive. Even bad news can be good news told in a positive manner. Just a smile on your face when telling bad news can make a difference.

Try going home to the family with the world on your shoulders, you will find some of your own family asking what is wrong, than saying they had it worse, while others will steer clear of you. Go home with a smile and your conversation that evening will be much better.

The in-your-face hyper maniac has extreme highs and lows when going home, while the stealth has a

Mania, Mania, Mania

fewer extremes because he can trigger a more positive mental condition.

You have to decide to change but many are not able to, and it's even harder to keep being happy. As you will read later in this book, you have a home face and work face. They tend to tell different stories depending on your environment.

Think about it.
Have faith in what you do, without conviction there is no hope. How can you look a woman in the eye and talk of love without conviction?

Unless you are in-your-face!!! Then you do it all the time, leaving disaster and carnage all around thereafter.

Mania, Mania, Mania

We are all a little mad

Chipmunkapublishing has a strap line 'We are all a little mad' as opposed to 'You don't have to be mad to work here but it helps'.

It is a horrifying fact that one in four will suffer a mental condition at some time during their life. But you are not out of the woods yet!! These people are not confined to one village or town. They are mixed in with the rest of the community. Therefore they will have contact with others, bringing the numbers affected up to 3 in 4. No, I hear you say, well yes. These people go to work, have family loved ones and contact with the outside world. These people work as councillors, carers and support workers.

Borderline personality disorders group states 80% of all people have some form of personality disorder.

The numbers are too large to figure, so we are all little mad, but may not need for drugs.

It might start with stress at work or in the family, move on to poor eating due to lack of time, resulting in bad health then into a break down.

Baby blues is too common in mothers that have just had a child. They can burst into tears for the smallest of reasons.

Mania, Mania, Mania

There are some good books on what can influence your mental health. It might not be you, it could be your environment.

But needless to say they can't lock us all up, because we are all a little mad.

Think about it.
With madness, there can be great things. The mental health of the world is totally unstable. There is too much excessive drinking and eating in some countries and not enough food and fresh water in others.

Mania, Mania, Mania

Environment, food and love

Environment is such an issue now. In some cases the government are doing a great job of keeping it as it was. In other cases enlightenment has left the building.

Follow the Chart line

Low job - low food - bad heath - low job - low money

Think about it.
Being poorly paid can mean eating poor food. In China the old wages were a Dollar a day and a bowl of rice. They did not worry so much about the money, the food kept them going.

However a high carbohydrate diet did mean low vitamins etc., leading to poor health.

Poor health can decrease the income because you only get paid for the days you work.

This decreases the amount of money you have to spend on food.

Mania, Mania, Mania

I would not advocate free food, but you can see chaos in a person's life caused by lack of it.

In India this leads to personal debt, the only solution to get out of this is to sell an organ! You can't do this too many times.

In New Orleans during Hurricane Katrina in 2005 people lost everything, only just keeping their lives. They will need state aid for many years or more to escape the poverty trap.

Think about it.
What do you say when 10,000 people plus have lost everything? They can't even go back to work!!

There are no shops to buy food, there is nothing. Even the water is bad for you.

The European governments are anti GM crops while it's a standard practice in the USA.

The old adage *'You can take a girl out of a trailer park but you can't take the trailer park out of the girl'* is true.

Mania, Mania, Mania

The natural resources of the world are running out. In the last 100 years we have used more than any other time.

We are becoming conditioned to live life faster, spend more consume more. In the UK, landfill is such an issue, while in the developing world they feed off others on rubbish.

If your environment is upsetting you change your environment.

Think about it.
Some people in Europe, North America and other places can move out. But what happens if you have to live next to a coalmine and your health suffers because of coal dust. Or you live in the jungle where the creature that can kill you, will.

If you grow up in a society that promotes sleeping around or having unprotected sex, then you move out before you become a victim of your environment. Everything is becoming consumed, not used, loved or looked after.

Think about it.
We live in a country where unprotected sex is on the increase. So is underage birth.

Mania, Mania, Mania

Sleeping around sounds nice, however it leads to a number of issues: unwanted babies, sexually transmitted diseases (STD) and low self-esteem. Sex therefore becomes a consumer item, just like a transaction, and less of an emotion.

The middle class follows this Food chart

Own food - Mass produced - organic

Feudal farming gives way to mass production and then people look for organic produce in the supermarket.

As discussed you are what you eat, you do not need a dietician to work out what is good for you. You need not have those expensive pills; in fact good eating is the order of the day. Look at people who have low incomes; their bodies can be in better condition because they are living off the ground.

For example, in Latvia McDonalds lose money - not only is their product new to the people, but also it costs double a good meal in the traditional eating-houses.

Some of the new European countries can show a thing or two to those old countries. They have practised organic farming and not moved on to intensive farming, while everywhere else is trying to

Mania, Mania, Mania

become organic because that's what the buying public ask for. The UK organic food market is increasing by 12% a year, while the margin for such a product is 20% higher than mass marketed product.

There is no surprise that after the foot and mouth cases in the UK, farmers received a good payout from the state. They still wanted to be in farming however realised that the UK was not the place to be. They sold their land at £8,000 per acre and moved to Latvia, Lithuania etc buying land for £200 per acre. Not that they really worked on the farms but they had a low cost business under easier conditions.

Even the air you breathe is food to your body, giving you energy. However, in the developing world there is an increase in asthma as the air becomes polluted. Crops have too many nitrates and phosphates.

The size of the average European waist is on the increase and this due to social conditioning (let's eat fast food), poor diet (more fast food) or too much money (put it on the plastic.)

Think about it.
There was a need to increase production of foods. However, organic sales in North

Mania, Mania, Mania

America and Europe increase by 15% a year.

You are what you eat. So what are you eating?

You and your environment are linked in ways that you really might not see. However spoil your environment and you have spoilt what you eat.

Mania, Mania, Mania

Love

Mania has different forms of affection.

In both cases (Hyper & Hypo) you have to be trusted by the person. While a family context is very hard within a work context it is easier. Later we will talk about fools and relationships. Both (Hyper & Hypo) are low contact for high periods of time, there is more compassion to the person and their physical and mental condition. Often they take higher moral ground that other people.

The stealth hyper maniac will see personal gain as a long experience, while the in-your-face will need to see a win in a short period of time, otherwise he will not be interested.

To gain respect is harder with the stealth type because while they appear relaxed on the outside they trust very few people on the inside. However you can gain more respect with the in-your-face type by conceding ground. Not seeing or hearing from either party is not a bad thing. With the stealth type once respect is established the conversations are meaningful and secure, unlike other groups where it's all false.

The stealth type tend not to play with people's emotions. They can steer you in a direction, but often they are more willing to give you more rope to

Mania, Mania, Mania

hang yourself. But only the stealth will nearly always pull you in.

In-your-face, will build you up only to drop you.

They understand personal development, for those they trust they will let you make calculated mistakes. They debrief you on where it went wrong. They might even put themselves up as a fool (discussed later) to learn more about you, your contacts or the way to work.

They love in a hands-off manner, not saying words like 'I love you' or having external affection, but rather knowing they have a person that cares for them. A good book to explore this is *Cultures and Organisations* (Profile Books, ISBN 1861975430).

Think about it.

The in-your-face type have no love in them, they consume sex, passion and people. These types change lovers as often as they change their underwear (if they wear any).

You will see that a Bi-polar might be in the middle ground between manias. They will only settle with someone they can not only trust but are also equal to.

Mania, Mania, Mania

Stealth - they need to trust and be equal and then they are in many cases a partner for life. They have in the main monogamous relationships; they feel they do not need to look around.

This is a good time to talk about right and wrong, is it OK just because others have sex? Is it OK if in a certain culture that you are gay until you are 21, then you get a girl friend?

Is it OK? You work it out!!

Mania, Mania, Mania

Going nowhere?

You think your life is going nowhere?

Both groups do things for a reason. The stealth person would clean toilets or do manual work just to see how something works. These people do not fear death so the types of jobs they do could be dangerous.

While in-your-face, waits for a low, to build you to a high, only to be dropped again.

Stealth like detail (to different extents), if they can't do it they pass the job on to someone they can trust (stealth) . You might not have seen someone with hyper mania for some time or heard their name in the news. Not because they have done things in a bad way but more because they are getting ready to move on.

Too much of one thing can spoil it. Jamie Oliver had been seen everywhere for 6 months. He needs to step out and come back.

In Hollywood there is a balance between stepping out and just not coming back. John Travolta was not mainstream for 20 years, but when he came back he did it big style.

Mania, Mania, Mania

A hyper maniac will see opportunities, you might not hear of them but they are there in the background.

There are times when a person can burn out or drop out (discussed later). They can bounce back or fall into depression.

Your life might look as if it is going nowhere, but it is. If you do not understand then you should, otherwise crawl back under that rock.

Think about it.

There is a vast difference between the two types.

One plans therefore does not fail, the other fails to plan therefore fails.

There is a focus with the stealth - they will only appear to be doing a low-paid job for a reason.

The in-your-face will be doing it because he has no money and his self-esteem has been really knocked.

Mania, Mania, Mania

Chameleons

It takes on average between 5 seconds and 30 minutes for a stealth   to blend in.

An example of this was in Boston, USA when the passing traffic was asking **me** for directions. Blending in is what a stealth does best. Even within their own family they can often be invisible, because they can be (stealth only) . By blending in they get more information and can assimilate to the situation fast.

In-your-face can not blend in, even if he is a room of his own kind.

Only when the environment is mixed can you start to flush them out. Another example was in London at a prize giving for publishing awards. The people at the table I was on were so convinced that I owned a bank of magazines. They started to split the beans on circulation issues. The information gained quickly and moved a business on, when challenged about revenue streams a fully paid constant could not have done better (an example of information gathering).

The more often that they go out the better they are at cloaking themselves. Their highly retentive memory helps them to either feed back the same data in a different way or spin out a conversation to distract attention away from themselves. Where

Mania, Mania, Mania

they do not know the subject of conversation they intently study the person talking and learn from them.

The in-your-face sticks out like a sore thumb and if he is not centre of attention then something is up. He needs to be in the thick of things. He might not have attractive women around him but he will already know who is attending the venue and who he needs to talk to. He will not be blunt, because he knows how to keep relationships on the level. But if you are on his hit-list watch out, he will extract all he needs.

During a recent trade show, a chap from India came on the stand with two others. He was dismissed by the owners but when after 30 seconds he said 'I want that product' and further still kept on coming back. He was a wealthy person with great ideas, but sold to as if a resident of Mumbai was selling to him, talking about dialects and areas along with the caste system. Only a stealth can do this effectively. His projects could increase the company's net profit tenfold.

Understand the people you are talking to, it does help.

You need to decide what the purpose of the meeting is otherwise these people will drive you wild.

Mania, Mania, Mania

Think about it.

The in-your-face cannot blend in, that's why they stick out like a sore thumb.
You can see a fast car, flash watch or designer cloths.

The stealth dresses for the occasion - he will have a feel of the dress code and blend to it.

A chameleon blends in well, as do the stealth. However an in-your-face would only blend in when there is a room full of in-your-face, all posturing, each one with a better story of the untold.

In the late 1980's there was in the cities of London and New York a game called wod. The trader with the smallest amount of cash in their wallet paid for the drinks, and these drinks were not cheap (rich become richer and poor become poorer). This was before credit cards.

Then the next step was the highest credit limit on credit cards.

Mania, Mania, Mania

In all these games you do not blend in, you stick out. This leads to traders being robbed of their cash.

Mania, Mania, Mania

The one to watch/sleight of hand

Both types will use sleight of hand to different degrees. Some will say you are strategic, a key partner or important to the business. It's that NLP stuff again, others will love bomb you (spend so much time with you that you just can't think).

The only difference is the complexity of the tick. A good hyper maniac will split off the strong first and undermine them (not attack) in such a way that they have to follow divide and conqueror, the weaker ones will be forced to follow. These methods are covered later in Sun Tze and Genghis Khan.

The stealth hyper maniac will spend more time herding the cats (or people) into order, while the in-your-face will have two or three different candidates lined up.

A frequent trick used by the hyper maniacs is public confrontation in front of an office. Things like "you are with me, are you not James." Poor James can't get out of agreeing otherwise he will be ripped apart by the hyper maniac. Being put down by a hyper maniac is not good, even worst of he is an in-your-face type.

I have used sleight of hand many times. I was asked to evaluate a business by a friend and I realised that this was pyramid selling by the

Mania, Mania, Mania

website. I decided to test the person (this is how hyper maniac let off steam, more later). The person called me on my mobile I said that I was on my way to a meeting by foot. They had 5 minutes. I really had 30 minutes. I asked what they know of my friend, they know only his name (great) and I then began to listen. He asked me what I thought of the online presentation. I said not "a lot"; I then began to take full control the situation. This is when sales people lose control of the situation, when confronted by a hyper maniac. After 30 minutes not only did I have him agreeing that this business was unsuitable for my friend but also questioning what he was involved. Most of the time an in-your-face hyper maniac will control the conversation. This does not happen when a stealth hyper maniac wants something else. They control the format and direction, but not always the words.

Think of a hyper maniac's mind in the form of snooker. They know the outcome and objectives, they do not mind conceding red balls or other colours if they have to. But if they want they can (and do) score maximum break. How? They line up all the balls and are a few shots in front.

Think of a carpenter's mate, during the last few years before he goes off on his own a good one will be two steps ahead on the job. He will know how many screws he will use, when to leave a section of glue to go off and where to work next. He will be thinking on his own but under the protection of the

Mania, Mania, Mania

main carpenter. Once he has does this he is ready to go out. If he goes out unprepared then his business will fail, who invites a cowboy back to do bad work?

Hyper maniacs plan - boy, do they plan. The numbers of alternatives are also in their mind. They have five plans while a normal person has one. In a conversation they can take full control answer questions before you think of them.

They are so flexible they will keep you guessing. They often send fools off on wild goose chases. Or out to do their research because the fool is convinced it's a great idea. They are unlikely to get drunk or start a fight.

Think about it.

The difference here is the over in seconds magic trick, to close a deal or sleep with someone.
Against planned attack, this might have taken months to plant but all of the ducks are in a row, and ready to be deployed. The latter will use red herrings to put people off the scent and also time the execution to their needs, not the need of others. It is often planned for the progress onwards.

Mania, Mania, Mania

Time out

We all need time out. The in-your-face more than the stealth hyper maniac.

I have experienced in-your-face sales people fall apart. This chap, let's call him Lain, was on the top of his career (not his personal life) and had an income of over £150,000 plus expenses. I was known within his industry as an over achiever. Heaven help you if you stood in his way. I subsequently met two people that were pushed within three weeks of their first confrontation. Lain's issue was that he had bad personal relationship skills (a trait of in-your-face) and that you had to pay homage to him or he stabbed you in the back.

Lain progressed from sales person to sales director, his personal turnover supported the company. The company grew and his income did with it. However Lain became a victim. He was so in-your-face that one June he told the chairman "Give me any target I will beat it". So the chairman did, he was after all riding on Lain's results. This was a bad time of year, fake jobs where booked in the order book was full but the factory empty. By August there was no work in the factory and the work in progress showed a good month. Lain's reign was shattering to end. In September the factory moved and started with a clean sheet. There were now two directors: Lain and a chap called Don. Over the next six months Lain lost

Mania, Mania, Mania

credibility with the board and ended up in the office for 6 months rather than gardening leave. They needed to know where he was. His mental state was totally shot, one day he spent all day like a three year old in a room with no TV or phone banging a tube on the table.

His next role three months after was on a pittance of a salary because the trade found out that he was let go for not achieving targets set.

Stealth hyper maniacs are better off if they hit the bottom. They tend not to get depressed by working themselves up to a better position. They are more controllable of their emotions therefore and pick out a role that looks good on paper.

Would you rather employ someone that's been let go and has adverse press or someone with average results? The latter always wins until the former gets his house in order.

Back to NLP, the amount of time out positively is equal to the amount of control the person has over himself or herself. Therefore if a person of either type can control their emotions then they are more likely to have longevity of employment and stable relationships (more later).

Mania, Mania, Mania

Think about it.

In-your-face will be at top speed most of the time; they only have time out when they have burnt out. This is when they are low and can be attacked.

Stealth will use the unexpected holiday or even day to take time out. If you study your subject, they normally take time out doing something different rather than sitting down.

More recently you can see them doing charity work, or helping others. This does tend to give them away, more than they like.

Mania, Mania, Mania

Learning

A hyper maniac learns even while in a car, they use NLP.

NLP is all about programming your mind and the mind of others.

The hyper maniac, as stated earlier, is always a few steps ahead. They have a vision. This must be how they do it! Sometimes it does not matter who gets in the way, sometimes they might be so ahead of the market it's a worry.

I picked up a report in September last year about e-books. They were soon to expand onto the global market, while they had been around for some years: the internet helped the sales.

I did my research over the following months and found out the market price and the suppliers of the service. The standard offering was restrictive so I made the product an easier offering.

After a one-hour presentation to the CEO, he allowed me to trail 5 books on Amazon and 20 on our own site. After 5 months the project was passed breakeven and 95% of sales are from the website not Amazon. The book trade even tries to order these books because their system does not know what they are.

Mania, Mania, Mania

You might learn but you have to apply it, see shoot the MBA.

Once you have mastered that NLP stuff, you can learn anywhere.

Hyper maniacs are very focused on reading. I only read book and papers that are targeted to my reading. Don't worry hyper maniacs like football rugby and other sports. They are very focused.

If a hyper maniac wants to know more about a business model or method of working, they will find out. They can gather information (as discussed already).

Think about it.

The difference can be from one extreme to the other unless they have moved from in-your-face to Stealth.

In-your-face is only as good as the last conquest. If there is luck, then he might have a great amount of loans, but he is solvent.

The progression from in-your-face to stealth will have a poor secondary education,

Mania, Mania, Mania

however qualifications in later life. They realise that education has a value.

Stealth, they are too educated. They might have three honours degrees and a number of masters degrees. Holding a conversation with them on any subject could be hard.

They are often too qualified and any CEO with a brain cell would know that they could do their job much better.

However it's not the pressure of the CEO, it's the limelight they might find hard.

There are few examples of Stealth becoming In-Your-Face but it does happen. The trigger is the taste of power, however they do become a hybrid version, not the fully polarised version, with traits in both camps.

Mania, Mania, Mania

Fear & greed

Hyper maniacs know that fear and greed drive people. However they are not normally concerned about death, this makes them stronger.

For example, millions enter the lottery to win. However a hyper maniac knows that the odds are not in their favour. There are many scams on the net. The best ones offer 15% of someone's bank account. All you have to do is take the money into your account and then split it up. People are up for this, greed takes over, all that all they can see is the money. The scam is to take an admin fee from you of £1,000 (Nigeria 317 letter scam), this scam is so bad in the UK SO19 has been set up to monitor it. There are 20 body bags sent back from the country that operate the scam every year. Don't worry on the other end the scammer is in fear of tier life. If they miss the target they get a trip to the seaside (not nice) they are pushed off the cliff to the sharks.

Next time to see an e-mail from a man (or woman) offering you a slice of $50Million, you will know what they are trying to do.

At my brother's wedding his best man feared him because he had a water pistol filled with a liquid. He was in fear because he has always been in fear and not taken control.

Mania, Mania, Mania

The greed is something most sales people are told to use in presentations, however our hyper maniacs use it to great effect. Both directly and indirectly, they will build up a database of greed or fear triggers.

For example I have met people that find being out of a relationship hard, they get off with someone just to be in a relationship. These people are easily corrupted into going off with the other sex, even if they do hate them.

Products are sold on fear and greed. Look at Viagra, which is sold on the fear of losing someone and greed for longer sex.

Fear and greed appeal to our animal instincts as well: the more controlled you are the less fear and greed control you.

A good hyper maniac (Stealth) will control himself or herself enough to say to an attractive person, 'No thank you, I am happily married.' Or stay off drinking for long enough to learn from the drunken customers around them. While the in-your-face will be up for both.

The less controlled a person is the more leverage you have with fear and greed.

Mania, Mania, Mania

Think about it.

Control of others (including the situation) is what both types do. However this is where the similarities end. Because one will pressurise you into moving with you. The other will move the environments so you have to jump where they say.

You need to see it in action to realise how it works. The main driver of the in-your-face is extreme fear or greed, while stealth will make it very subtle.

Mania, Mania, Mania

Coming to terms with Mania

You can see that hyper mania is all around you. You might admit now that you are a hyper maniac or suspect a friend or relative.

We have covered many aspects of the condition but you need to start learning more about these people.

Coming to terms is easy, all you have to admit is that you are a hyper maniac. It's like having your first credit card. Do you use it carefully or do you blow it all?

The answer to that question is whether you are stealth or in-your-face. If you are in-your-face you will blow the lot, get leisure and enjoy. Stealth puts the card in a safe place after making a single transaction (small) just to test out how it works.

Now you are starting to get the picture we can move on to learning about NLP.

This is like your personal choke chain, you can learn to turn your emotions off. Once you have done this your will be very effective and dangerous.

Mania, Mania, Mania

Think about it.

Controlling mania is the key.

The sooner you come to terms with it, in which ever for you might have the better, even if you are Bi Polar then there is very little planning you might have to prepare you.

There is even less on in your face or Stealth. These are not really medical conditions that might be covered by a GP. If you manage to see a GP, they might just give you Prozac or something to clam you down.

Denial of mania in a personal or family situation is common. Trying to explain a situation that you are not qualified on or understand nothing about is also an issue.

Mania, Mania, Mania

You can do it all with Mania

Just like PCP, you can with hyper mania. PCP or angel dust is sold in the USA. The police carry pump action shot guns because they shoot the limbs of people taking PCP. The super human strength comes from within, for stealth hyper maniacs and from the audience (or expected audience) for the in-your-face.

You could almost reprogram yourself, get control of you life and have everything your heart desires. If you are privileged enough to go to an Anthony Robbins' conference you could walk on fire or snap wood with your hands.

Once you have set your mind and actions, the rest is easy.

It is that simple, positive mental attitude does it all. Strong will power is not to be underestimated, if you enjoy smoking and need to give it up then change the way you think about smoking. Instead of looking forward to a smoke think about a negative, the cost, the harm to your body or the fact that you smell like an ashtray. This mental thought will help your smoking decrease or stop, as you inhale the smoke you are filling your lungs up with tar, this mental picture will put you off smoking.

This is a simple form of NLP.

Mania, Mania, Mania

Think about it.

You cannot buy mania in the shops!!!

There are a few ways to get it, but I am not going to tell you what triggers it. Other than the external environment, look at New York, full of one type.

I can tell you what triggers Bi Polar - drugs - such as Cannabis, Coke and E - have spoilt lives of the individual and their family. This has created more than Bi Polar, the by-product can erode a person's mental health.

Furthermore drugs (Prozac etc) do not cure everyone, they can only cure a number of cases. Why? Because the individual needs to understand himself or herself first before they can communicate effectively the issues they need addressing.

Talk therapy has been more affective than drugs. As the self esteem increase, due to the interaction with a real person.

Mania, Mania, Mania

Talk therapy, demand good people who are qualified to do this type of work. Needless to say they are more expensive than drugs and also you need more of them. However they are very effective and have good longterm results.

Mania, Mania, Mania

I have a direction, decide yours

As I have already stated, I know what I have to do, and I will. This is normal for a hyper maniac, but just the direction for stealth and in-your-face are different.

In sales, they are called hunters and farmers. The hunters go after the kill while the farmer grows his crop with loving care. In some cultures they are only hunters, if they have not had a kill for some time then the family could starve. Look at parts of Asia; they live off rice, there would not be enough meat to feed the population.

Planning your route is very important. While a journey starts with the first step, what if it's in the wrong direction? We plan to win, but some fail to plan.

Stealth joins up the dots in the plan created, while in-your-face take the direct route.

The book is full of personal experience and thoughts pulled in from being hyper maniac, yet also understanding the different flavours of hyper mania.

Now is a good time to reflect.

Mania, Mania, Mania

You can do a SWOT, or similar or just relax and think about what you have done and what you want to do.

The only thing holding YOU back is YOU.

Think about it.

You need to know what you are doing.

The in your face, has no direction. They blow with the wind. If they could see more money from another activity they will go that way.

Stealth plans for good times and bad times. They do plan in advance.

Mania, Mania, Mania

You will always be

A hyper maniac, unless you use NLP to make yourself boring.

You see you might enjoy living on the edge or being behind some famous people. Or you might be the best sales person in the world.

You will always be:

- a son or daughter
- husband or wife
- father or mother
- worker or boss
- singer or dancer

But you will always be you

Think about it.

You are a person; you have to live with it. Because others will remember you for who you are and what you did.

Mania, Mania, Mania

Think and question

Being a hyper maniac will teach you to question everything.

It is not dependant on which type you are but rather that it's in your programming. You will evaluate (or learn to) for yourself, yes you will make mistakes but you are doing your own risk assessment of the situation.

For example, I was invited to join a company whose practices were just about legal, while the salary was great and the so-called prospects good. They needed me more that I needed them, on the first interview they asked only about me. When I asked about the job they simply said we will come back to that. I had done my homework and found out how they operated. After asking about the role, the office conditions more than four times. I said is it true that you're a life insurance broker? That you are looking for me to become an independent principle to sell polices to my network of contacts? The interviewer said no we are a professional company operating in the insurance market. Anyway you appear not to be suitable. I found out later that it's not until the fifth interview they tell you about the company you see you have to be manageable (or gullible).

By doing your homework you decrease your exposure to adverse press. This is vital for the in-

Mania, Mania, Mania

your-face sales person. It also means you hit the ground running, you know their markets, the company strengths and normally the office / company politics. We will cover this later.

You will also find this useful when going out to buy a house. Three years ago we wanted to move house. We went round with a clipboard, making notes on each property. We then used this data to make an offer; we know from the data that the house might cost £200,000 but the repairs £50,000. Therefore the true cost is £250,000. We found a house where we knew what to expect.

This can also be applied to contacts you might have come across, what is their agenda? Why do they want a formal meeting? You will find that hyper maniacs hate time wasters and hate to waste time themselves.

An example is in one company I had worked in. Run by an in-your-face hyper maniac, sales meetings lasted 2 minutes per person plus 30 seconds at the end. All the chap wanted to know was what you had achieved last week, what you expected to do this week. He would use double entry on a book and as long as the total figure was correct then he was happy. And if he was not he would give the group a mouthful.

An elephant is one big animal to eat; however you can eat him step by step. You set up phased

Mania, Mania, Mania

objectives to reach, and reach them you do. And you will eat your elephant; it's traditional for the in-your-face sales person to be head hunted every 18 months (bad ones every 6 months). This means that they can either move on or stay and increase their salary.

While very good at their job, both types of hyper maniacs will leave employment in a creative way, thus letting the system work for them. I have booked a holiday for 14 days, then sent an e-mail to resign or given 2 days notice. Planning or timing is everything: the in-your-face sales person will move and take work with him; the stealth sales person takes the better customers and leaves a factory full of low margin high effort work.

The impact to the new business will be great, to the old business, hell.

You have to question everything:
- you
- your environment
- what you want out of life

THEN you have to do it, not plan, **do it.**

Think about it.

In your face does not think it's from the gut. They do not look before they jump.

Mania, Mania, Mania

Mania

As discussed already, with stealth it's timing and what you do not say. In a recent meeting I was not interested in what was being said, but rather the pecking order. This enabled me to go directly to the boss and focus my questions on him.

The Conservative party campaign in 2005 was controlled by stealth, the number of seats reduced by employing the Australian election guru. His actions and his historic campaigns did make a difference.

Stealth hyper maniacs, like plants, hate staying in the spot light. They much prefer the shade. They are best at controlling the situation for someone else. They make exceptional mentors. I often get the 60 second call: it might be we have been offered 50 free staff, how can we use them? Or how can we increase our market share? They see things in shades of grey but also black and white.

A true example happened in March 2005 when I had a call from an IT specialist. He really wanted to see how I was. He was concerned about his presentation on a multi million pound install contact. The presentation was to a channel supplier, not the end customer. We discussed his proposition for 55 minutes and changed his presentation so much he rewrote it but won the business. For him the

Mania, Mania, Mania

hardest part was overcoming payment. The example I gave was:
A man fills up his car with petrol; you are the petrol pump attendant (or cashier) and you have to make sure he pays for the goods. But how does he pay? Cash (because its burning a whole), credit card (because he has no cash), fuel card (it's not his car) or any number of other means. You see it's not up to you how he pays but rather that he does pay. You can't interface directly; your approach has to be compassion. You can help him by saying, that's 30 quid, do you have your credit card (assumptive close).

But when dealing with corporations that need products, they normally leave the payment to the FD, on the books, off the books, sales and lease back, sold to sister company or just pure cash. You need to understand your customer and their situation.

Wars are won by going out for it and by stealth. One only does not work but together the war will be won.

Think about it.

People with Mania do not sit on their bottoms, or work in a factory doing endless boring things.

Mania, Mania, Mania

Life's rich tapestry

Why the hell do we do the things we do?

There are those that do what they want to and those that do what they have to. If you are a hyper maniac you do what you have to.

Because hyper maniacs are learning all the time they are just like cows, they digest information four ways. They gather information and sort it or dump it. You might meet a hyper maniac and think what a sad git. But when you need information who do you go to? That sad git or guru?

It lies in the rich tapestry because it makes a pattern and the pattern is there for a purpose. It shows the real you. Hyper maniacs as discussed before tend to use perception and reality rather well. There are ways to flush out the real them but if you look at what they have done and how they have done it, it shows their true colours. A word of warning is that hyper maniacs can tend to leave a number of contacts without knowing each other. They keep high level contacts together and these are not mixed with family members.

An example of an in-your-face hyper maniac gone wrong. This chap I spent 9 months in a shared office with, was call Alistair. Both his business and personal life were a disaster. He had the gift of the gab and was a good salesman selling a high value

Mania, Mania, Mania

product. However he knew nothing, he had to set up a different business every 7 months because he spent all of the money. He left in his wake 6 investors nursing £200,000 in never-to-be-seen again investments (losses). His personal life was worse when he got bored with a woman so he left her and started with another: 4 wedding cakes and 7 kids later. He decided to settle down with a Russian girl, but little did he know: 3 years later she would leave him with her nice English passport. The picture he left was full of holes.

You might feel it's two steps forward and ten steps back, but life does that sometimes. You need to start with a good foundation.

Think about it.

You only get one life, the in your face do appear to have a roller coaster ride, but you only get one.

You can leave riches or a wasteland behind you. The choice is yours.

Mania, Mania, Mania

Relationships

These in a person's life are important; no one likes to be left alone. If you are about to start relationships as a hyper maniac, choose a wife that understands, be faithful to her and you will have a solid foundation.

She will have a choice, steady (bad) income or the unexpected. If she can cope with the unexpected then you can't go too far wrong.

I have a loving caring wife, I spent ten years in a 24/7 environment. I could call up at 9pm on Friday and say I will be back tomorrow. It's not that I was down the pub but rather that I was at work earning money. Most days I would get into work (not leave) by 7am and leave by 7pm (12 hour days), sometimes I would leave for work at 3am, you see, hyper maniacs do not require too much sleep. Just drive to get the job done. This is one of the factors that make hyper maniacs different.

To take the pressure off my wife I bottle fed our children at 5am, this meant they would sleep until 8am and she would have a lie in. As they developed, they would not get respect until it's earned. We have one TV in our house, not because we are poor but rather to get three children to learn to agree. Attached to the TV are a PlayStation, Sky and a DVD. They have to agree (they are 7 years apart) the play station has been taken away due to

Mania, Mania, Mania

bad school results (up to 5 weeks) and has nearly been binned 8 times in one year. The Sky is only the basic package and has been turned off twice for 3 weeks. By only having one TV they have to communicate (includes arguments) with each other. They do have toys in their bedroom however they have a strict father and mother.

Other kids that come to our house have a TV in their room and a floor full of broken toys. I just follow the example of my upbringing. However when we go out I am often that proud of my kids, others I have seen are just animals. Some call it conditioning.

At the weekend we do Saturday and Sunday jobs, visiting relatives. My children know that they can't get out of them and they do them due to obligation and respect. There are plenty of children that have no respect for their parents or elders, this is bad.

Where they are family (or extended family) and you have no time for them, STAY away. I have no respect for my mother in law, in fact I call them the big kids (this is the way hyper maniacs ridicule people), they are worst than my 89 year old grand mother that we see on Sundays. They ring up because they have run out of milk, loo roll or need to talk to someone. They are a pain, when they once looked after my 8 year old I thought she was in charge.

Mania, Mania, Mania

As they say if you want to be wise stay with wise people.

The more you as a hyper maniac know about relationships, the more variety of relationships you have. The key ones are your family, they are your focus on earning income; love them or not they, are your family.

The in-your-face or hypo maniac is less concerned about relationships. These are more deposable; he consumes people so fast he is onto the next before they know it.

Think about it.

You can either waste a relationship or watch it develop; however it takes two to tango. You decide, however do you fancy divorce and leaving kids as victims'?

Mania, Mania, Mania

The cut off

There are times when you need to walk away, not stealing any lines from Kenny Rogers and coward of the county.

As a stealth hyper maniac I can tell earlier than an in-your-face hyper maniac and they can tell way before the normal man when to walk away.

It's as much about walking away as it is the way in which you do it. The stealth hyper maniac would ask for further gathering time and information on a project (from him). The in-your-face hyper maniac would turn the meeting round to get an agreement to meet at a further date once they have come back to him (to him).

They are control related: the stealth that they appear in control, the in-your-face that he is in control.

They do not like burning bridges, but when they want to, they do more than burn them. I have seen in-your-face sales people physically destroy servers. Just to keep the company from keeping the data, or write to each client with a better proposal.

DO NOT annoy a hyper maniac. They are like elephants, they never forget.

Mania, Mania, Mania

Think about it.

You do not want to upset either. They are like elephants.

They really do not forget. It might take days or months, but they will remember what you did for them.

With in-your-face a punch in the face often offends.

Mania, Mania, Mania

Blending life

Hyper maniac home life is different to work life. Even the in-your-face hyper maniac does not want too much confrontation at home.

My children are great at misinformation, disinformation and deception. However they can't use it too often on each other, because they can see it coming. Having worked from home they do tend to pick up words or phases.

Being a hyper maniac is not all work, there is the fun aspect. You need to take time out and time with your family. You also need time away from the fools that surround you (to be discussed later).

Even a train does not go full speed all of the time; learn to take time out. You will find this a great period to learn….

Think about it.

Once you have come to terms with your mania you need to make it work. This is much harder for in-your-face, because they have all the finest of elephant poo.

Mania, Mania, Mania

Ring fencing

As you grow older you will feel the need to ring-fence relationships, not that you are hiding anything, but rather so you do not have to explain action to both parties.

Try not to be in someone else's pocket or you have a mutually exclusive life. This means you have a critic that might not understand your objectives or the bigger picture.

This is more familiar with women, but can happen with drinking partners.

By each group being exclusive you are not mixing family and work. My father was against me being involved in the family business and I am happy that I was not, I am my own man.

By ring-fencing, you become a different person. I once worked in an open plan office and this chap called Jason was the hard man, he took no stick. He started up a relationship with a pretty young lady. However, the hard man dropped every time she called on his mobile. He became a sweet young sex kitten.

By ring-fencing you are using your chameleon techniques.

Mania, Mania, Mania

Think about it.

You need to keep personal/family different from that of work.

They all have a different way of thinking about you. Your family could retell times when you have embarrassed yourself; this might not be good for work mates.

In-your-face, puts them all in a room, expects them to get on and buys them drinks all night.

Sorry! Life is not like that.

Mania, Mania, Mania

Turning off

We all need to turn off and spend time with the ones we love or doing what we love. However an in-your-face hyper maniac can turn off more than a stealth hyper maniac.

If playing or looking at football, we need to get into the game, however hyper maniacs are good at dual tasking. They will let the brain work slowly through something subconsciously while the conscious is doing the activity.

The turning off is often considered as sport, however once you have been a hyper maniac you will find what it is. Normally for the stealth hyper maniac it's not drink, for the in-your-face it might well be drink. Find your ways of unwinding, this is key to relaxing.

The creator and founder of boo.com used extreme sport. He loved skiing (most in-your-face do); the fact that he concentrated on saving his skin meant that he could turn off from work.

There is often a band or track of music that might help; those calming music CDs are good for some. It might be a walk in the park or a power jog. Find out what it is and do it.

Mania, Mania, Mania

However it is not getting drunk, or sleeping around, or drugs. This is mind, body and soul unless you are a hypo maniac (in-your-face).

Think about it.

You do not need drugs.

The body produces enough of its own.

Mania, Mania, Mania

Cutting out

As already discussed, your environment feeds you. Most hyper maniacs tend to cut out coffee or caffeine based dinks. They do have them when they need to.

They like to reduce fast food and prefer orange juice to fizzy drinks. They know that their body is their main tool for an income.

They also tend to have fewer days off sick because they eat healthier food. Though they tend not to be vegans, just careful of what they eat. Many take trips to the gym or find ways of keeping fit.

Cutting out still refers to mind body and soul. I am happy to have given up drinking 20 odd years ago. Not that I do not want people to have a few drinks, but rather I am not worried about being stopped for drinking and driving. I do not wake up with a hang over or any of those things.

Too much of anything is bad for you; I will not waste four more trees with a chart, if you understand, then cut it out.

Your mind body and soul will improve as will your pocket. This amount of difference can really be surprising.

Mania, Mania, Mania

Do nothing to excess; too much of anything is bad for you. There are some vitamin C drinks that can change the colour of your skin if you have too much of them.

Think about it.

Look after yourself; there is only one you. If you spoil it, you spoil you.

Mania, Mania, Mania

Kids

They are a by-product of you!!! Only recently has Haynes, the car people, produced a manual for kids.

After the age of two the child will start to do what you do, they do it first to copy you. Then it will haunt you. It's all part of their environment and conditioning, they take both the good and bad. Beware, they are a mini you.

You have the God-like power to mould these offspring into the fully rounded person. You could also spoil their lives.

Some Hollywood types are either fully exposing their kids to their lifestyle, wars and all, others hide their family until 16 or 18 from the media.

The PlayStation generation can multitask. From an early age they can start to process information faster, looking at the game play, maps and figures at the same time. They use e-mail, MSN and iPods all at the same time.

This skill should be used to move things on, start with Zoo Tycoon. This user-friendly environment gives them money and animals. They will get a feel for marketing prices and business.

Mania, Mania, Mania

Then if you can, build up to Age of Empires, Age of Mythology, Stronghold and then Jurassic Park and Operation Genesis. These games focus on evolving your culture and then dealing with the unexpected (loose animals).

Move up to Rome Total War (£25 games, £120 graphics card). This will teach them the type of troops and where to put the troops, and how to conquer.

By using these games in education rather than relaxation, you are starting to harden your kids. They have better duel processors, get them to apply what thy have learnt.

My five-year-old plays all of the above, does not understand most of it, but can play to a certain level. None are too bloodthirsty, but reflect culture and the makeup of society.

Kids are familiar with queues, go to any theme park and you think you are near the start. However you snake round and round until you reach the start of the queue.

While life is like this, it's just the perception that you are nearly there. This sense is increased as you can hear and see people enjoy them. Or a few minutes that you have been on the ride, you feel happy only to start the queue process all over again.

Mania, Mania, Mania

Where possible, take the kids aboard to learn a language or culture. This will round them off as a person. We are all stakeholders in society.

You need however to balance what you have, the issue is that if your kid is a bright spark you need to help him at every step of the way. You can't give a man a net because then he eats all of the fish. They must have a profiled education in progression; one year of good stuff followed by years of bad education can be to their detriment.

The under 18s with skills after all are the ones that are creating computer virus, mobile phone viruses and havoc. They are bored: do something about it before they do.

Do a little at a time; blend it in with bringing them up.

Use this power carefully, it does come back and bit you.

Think about it.

You might be surprised but kids grow up much faster.

Therefore education needs to be direct and in direct.

Mania, Mania, Mania

PC and PS 2 or 3 games that developed are great for Kids.
Starting with Zoo tycoon, which is about building a Zoo, looking after animals and the zoo money.

Even games like Rome total war are great because you can invade other countries. They need to learn the rules.

Take the cotton wool off you children, in their teens give them rope to developed and grow. Trust them as much as a parent can.

EACH GENERATION INCREASE THE AMOUNT OF COTTON WOOL, AND SPENDS MORE

Mania, Mania, Mania

Parents

Your parents have been and always will be your parents. Ok, you can do good or bad in their eyes, but they are still parents.

George w Bush and Barbara Bush must feel happy that their son is president. But he is still their son.

As a hyper maniac you are advised to hide what you do from these people, yes they might understand but since they wiped your bottom, fed and clothed you, they still know best (they think).

If you are in the shit or need their help go to them, but I learnt from the age of 16 they can be brutal and ask the most direct questions that cut through you.

My father was great; he would grill me about my next job, asking about the company, its funding, and methods to market, market, my role and so forth. You knew when he was disappointed but also when he was happy. They do love you, they might not show it but they do.
This issue is best covered by *Cultures and Organizations* ISBN: 1861975430

I have learnt that families in business are bad, the first generation make it, and the second generation CAN (but might not) improve it. The third generation just piss it up again the wall. Two

Mania, Mania, Mania

examples are the right way and the hell what happen to the business way.

The furniture company had been trading for 50 years, set up after the war it was a quality product made in the UK. Set up by two brothers it was a good company, by the time their two sons came to run the business it was still going strong. They had a passion for the business and where fundamentally good people. OK they had flash cars, but their eye slipped off the ball. They had a board meeting and the CEO was not a man of action. They put the business up for sale and sold it.

The printing company, great company set up by a printer for his family, his son moved the business on into a new age. This son was respected by all he met, no one had an unkind word: from the shop floor to the board, he had their respect. His son however bought in questionable business practices and surrounded himself with, yes, men. He lost the company $30m over 5 years and no one liked him; he even created a coup to get on the board of the holding company.

While neither company was listed, what would you do?

Within society, your link with your parents is strong.

Mania, Mania, Mania

Think about it.

Your relationship with your family can be strained. The normal family no longer exists, a number of people have a stepmother & stepfather, whom they really would rather not talk to.

The family unit has broken down; this CAN increase cases of mania and interdependencies'. Role reversal is now very common that mothers and fathers are more dependant on children and less dependant on themselves. The state offers little or no return.

Pensions from governments are too small to live on; even private pensions are not enough. There are people Globally working until they drop.

This disharmony affects everyone, creates a state of chaos. For his own personal gains, to the detriment of others.

In your face, will use this to divide and conquer, while stealth will try and bring the family unit back into harmony, or at the very least talking terms.

Mania, Mania, Mania

Extended family

My brothers and sisters are great, I like my father I am very blunt with them. If I say no I mean no.

You should treat your extended family like your parents; keep what you are doing to yourself. You have very little to live up to in their eyes.

Worse still, they might not see the bigger picture. If you are the best employer in the town you will always get "Please employ Jimmy, he is a good worker". If they are so good at running business they let them do it.

These people can be bigger critics of YOU, even worse than your parents because they are jealous. They want what you have, if you are an in-your-face hyper maniac then they see the good car and the international travel, not the hard work.

I fortunately have very few of these, but to those who do, get it sorted.

These are the very people who can erode your mind; I once took my children to work. I showed them my office, then went downstairs and spent 8 hours on a machine. They feedback to the extended family that I had an office and that I did work.

Mania, Mania, Mania

This is why a hypo maniac (in-your-face) moves out of town, they can take risks in a different town and still return to their own.

Think about it.

The extended family is by the same token becoming more misplaced. The number of people not talking to others has increased.

Seeing the common good has occurred, only in close nit communities is the extended family evident.

However this living in each other's pocket has an effect. Everyone knows your business; they expect to share in your worldly goods (car, house and land} because they have helped you get them. Within these communities in your face is thrown out or excommunicated, while stealth operates under the radar.

Within generations there is no real progress until you leave the community, because their view is similar to that of the family, you are still the son or daughter of X.

Mania, Mania, Mania

Getting the balance right

While stress costs the UK £100Bn a year and 3 in 1 visits to the doctor are because of mental health: do not be a victim.

Think about it.

You do not need, stress and stress junkies are bad. Your body was not designed for stress.

On a recent business trip, I met a very in tune person, who could see my mind racing but I still had my guard up. They spent 3 hours trying to understand me, however I was not prepared. NEVER share too much with a person at the first meeting.

Learn to get the balance right, if you are on a good income put up working with fools (discussed later). Then look to leave.

If you have issues with the family, then address them.

You might read a self-help book, but without applying the subject you might as well have not read it.

Mania, Mania, Mania

By addressing the personal balances you will be a better person. Sure the hyper maniac has issues to address and address them they must.

At the age of 17 I had a drink problem, I would go to the pub and drink as much as I could until the pub closed. At a party in 6 hours I drank a bottle of gin, a bottle of vodka and 16 cans of beer. I would have carried on but I was throwing up. I realised the next day what a fun party and that I had a drink problem. I spent the next week on one drink when I went out then quit drinking. Knowing that one pint would tip the balance to drinking again.

Do I miss it, no Hell. I do not waste money on drinks, if I am stopped by the police I know I can't lose my licence. My family knew that I stopped the next week and have not needed a drink since.
If I had carried on then I would have had a short life. It's now OK not to drink, but it was not 20 years ago.

**Address the issue before it addresses you!!
These can be addressed via NLP.**

Think about it.

Living on the edge only works for in your face types.

Mania, Mania, Mania

NLP for stealth is great; it really acts as a tune up. There is no balancing for the in your face, they are all or nothing.

Mania, Mania, Mania

Sleep

Like with many other things it's not the quantity but the quality. I know people that work a whole night shift and then sleep for only 3 hours.

Hyper maniacs tend to sleep for less than other people; they would prefer to work through an issue than sleep. 36-hour days are not unusual; in fact within the last 14 years they are the norm.

If you consider, the financial markets open in the Far East on Monday and close in the USA on Friday. There is a maximum of two hours that the markets are not trading and you will find hyper maniacs can do this for years. They are great traders.

Once you get to grips with your hyper maniac you will become attuned to your bodies needs. The better the quality of food and sleep, the better the output.

Think about it.

Your body does need rest. The in your face type does burn out rather quickly, while stealth can run for long periods without much sleep, they are in tune with their body so they can see the signs of sleep

Mania, Mania, Mania

depravation.

Mania, Mania, Mania

Sex

Hyper maniacs have a better loving relationship; some in-your-face hyper maniac might prefer quick relationships. But it's almost by mutual consent. They are looking for a life companion. Even past relationships are more about caring than sex.

While for the in-your-face it's more about conquest then move on.

Its not that they are unloving, more that they have an agenda.

Think about it.

In your face loves the conquest of sleeping around, why stealth is monogamous in relationships, this does not mean they do not talk to the opposite sex, but rather they do not see them as objects of sex.

It is interesting to note that the transition types are cause in between. They can progress from one side to the other.

Mania, Mania, Mania

Drugs

Stealth hyper maniacs tend to stay away from drugs, while in-your-face might use them for recreational purposes.

Think about it.

Drugs are a trigger, there has been a good debate on cannabis, and this has been proven to trigger long-term mental health issues. Leading to Bi polar, mania & psychosis.

The fictional character Sherlock Holmes would have been a hyper maniac. When he got bored (unchallenged) he would resort to opium.

Steer clear of drugs, these include caffeine. You might use caffeine as I do to keep you awake when you need to.

However please note that most drugs have side effects or knock on effects. Take vitamin v, the drugs that help men perform better. There is talk that one could make you blind, the other lasts for 36 hours and can cause gangrene. Both have been sighted for increased sexual desire, which affects your relationships. Which in turn affects everything else. Think of the poor woman who has to perform

Mania, Mania, Mania

every night for 4 years. She shortly must get fed up after the first few months.

The other issue is that the amount taken increases to give the same buzz. Think about beer or wine, how much you had to take to get drunk. It increases as your body gets used to the dose.

By taking drugs only when you have to, in effect, makes your body better. How can you or your body perform if you have been on a bender all night? You and your body rely on each other.

Take it carefully, you need your body, the side effects of what you are taking, might come back to get you after many years.

Drugs are down to cause and effect.

Think about it.

You will see in your face is often over the limit on drugs. Like beer and wine, they can often be fund with a line of coke too.

Stealth, might take drink in moderation, but is highly unlikely to take recreational drugs.

Mania, Mania, Mania

Uppers and downers

As a hype maniac you will need to be able to change your moods just using the body's own chemicals.

OK so it's more NLP, no sweat. You can trigger happy, objective and sad conditions just by simple things like music.

A few years ago an army commander was fined for speeding. He was listening to music in his car, hears the charge and instinct told him to charge, he did so.

In the USA an arm cadet was found guilt of shooting a group of people, before opening fire he had been conditioned to set off a whistle (which he did himself).

Watch your blood sugar level, this does drop like a stone with hyper maniac, you do not want to go hypoglycaemic.

You can push your body, but do not push it too hard. Find out what gets you down: it might be beer, nightclubs or credit card bills and cut it out.

Push body and mind too much and they will get back at you. While for the in-your-face this is not an issue, as he is always moving on. For the stealth it's always a concern.

Mania, Mania, Mania

Great Hypo maniacs (in-your-face) have years of great work followed by years of depression. The hyper maniac is far more stable. It's just like the rabbit and hare.

Learn what makes you happy and conditions your mind to focus.

Think about it.

You will see they mood swings on in your face every day.

I once saw one on gardening leaving, he was not trusted to stay at home; he would have run a side business. So the employer insisted that he came into the office, the first day he was offered a desk, however within hours he was causing issues with the staff, so they put him in a spare office.

However he made phone calls for the next hour (to customers saying he was leaving), so by the afternoon of the first day, he was placed in an office with no phone, just newspapers.

Mania, Mania, Mania

By the second day, he was in a vegetable state, and by the last day of the three-month gardening leave, he was nearly broken.

You can't trust them, so you need to break them; this is a similar situation to the army.

Mania, Mania, Mania

Love & marriage

To a hyper maniac love and trust are very similar.

Love is not instant, it can take time, however it can be over very quickly. Hyper maniacs tend not to show their real feelings. Only those close to the hyper maniac get to see the real person, expression of feeling.

Find someone who trusts YOU, I did, it counts.

Surely we have had our hard times, but the good ones have been great.

YOU have to ask them, would you prefer years of debt or the good life as we can afford it? If they really go for the latter then you COULD be Ok. Because while other people had flash cars my wife had a banger, but now she has a new car while others are worried about monthly payments.

To the in-your-face love and life are disposable. They move up and move on, often leaving a mess. This legacy does come back to find them.

Think about it.

In your face, is they type not to get into a relationship with, you are a toy and they will enjoy using you.

Mania, Mania, Mania

Mania in business

Unless you have a family pile, then you are in business for fun and for a living. Your business is YOU, not the products you handle or the deals you do, **it's you**.

People buy from people, they are buying from you. You might look good because your company or life style is flash, but they buy from you.

Business and family are best kept apart; let's get down to business.

Making a cup of tea the is like business

A fool boils the kettle many times forgetting what he is doing.
In-your-face gets someone to do it, they always do it, but badly (getting your own back).
TQM, has spent the last 5 years studying tea and has an optima production.
Six sigma has the full flow production.
Six sigma plus has water but only one tea bag left and that's for the wife. Without tea she is a bear with a sore head.

Mania, Mania, Mania

Think about it.

You will not see in-your-face making a drink unless it's in their interest to do so.

Commercial business is a competitive environment.

They like to use in your face to create new customers, because they are good at sales. Where client retention is down to Stealth, because they will keep the clients business.

I have seen in-your-face exceed his target by 1,000%, however there was no product in the warehouse. He was not selling; he was giving away, offering terms of 180 days and next day delivery, sale and return too.

Sales people in the from line often create fake customers, one door to door sales person signed up 350 new customers in a week, however all of the gas contracts where "fake". He just went through the telephone directory, and signed up everyone on the first page.

Mania, Mania, Mania

He left within 3 weeks, after 4 weeks the paperwork was rejected by the customers. Before he left he did get paid £5,900.

Mania, Mania, Mania

Building blocks

Everything you have learnt, directly or indirectly is a building block.

You might be young enough to remember your first driving lesson, sat behind the wheel of a killing machine. That also took you everywhere you wanted to go.

As your lessons increased so did your skill until you did not stall the car or hit the kerb. You could multi task with your mind.

These are the building blocks.

Where you start building and what you are building with are also an issue to address.

If you have good practical skills you do not want to be trapped in an office, if you have bad communication skills you do not want to start out as team leader.

I started out with 5 O levels & 1 A level selling chocolate, with a company. I was 19 with a company car. Within 9 months I would have been rep of the year.

You might have a bad environment, or be handicapped and reach this point sometime later in your life. It's not where you start as a hyper maniac

Mania, Mania, Mania

but it's where you are going to. This subject is covered further later on in the book.

You build to your own pattern, because what you are building reflects you. What I am building I know in my mind.

Think about it.

You do not get a life, you build it. Starting off in school then progressing to work.

In-your-face build on over achievement of the targets or conquests.

Stealth has a more measured approach.

<u>Consider your approach, what is it????</u>

Mania, Mania, Mania

Preparation

From building blocks you can prepare.

Once you have learnt to drive, you can prepare to go out into the big wide world. You need to plan where you are driving to, who you are going to see. You will need fuel, if you do not have fuel your need money. You might even need a present for the person you are seeing.

Proper **Planning** Prevents **Piss Poor** Performance: preparation is the key.

Like the journey, plan your life, not that you have your second child at thirty and your wife will be call Bo but outline what route you are looking to talk. Just like the car journey there could be a detour, as a hyper maniac you need to take this in your stride.

Anyone that has seen a professional at work will see that he is prepared. He will have a van full of tools and gear. A cowboy will come round with just a hammer. If you have seen Toy Story think of the professional that mends woody. He has everything, even the kitchen sink. You need to be like this, as a professional: if someone asks a question you need to come back quickly.

Mania, Mania, Mania

The in-your-face hyper maniac would sometimes shoot from the hip, with the stealth would sound off real facts.

The hyper maniac created the dotted pattern for his journey; the Hypo maniac goes hell for leather from A) to B) via the shortest route.

Plan, plan and plan again, beware plans change. But you won't, your route is set for your journeys.

Think about it.

You need to plan.

In your face, will jump in feet first expecting others to support him.

Stealth will have five options in their head, and four left field issues. Knowing there is not one answer, he might have many.

The greatest combination is for in your face to present and for stealth to support.

Therefore there is a fast slick presentation, with most of the answers at the team's fingertips.

Mania, Mania, Mania

However you will find that, most of the receiving team would post presentation want to deal with stealth.

Why, because he has the answers in a very straight way.

Mania, Mania, Mania

Analyse

Part of your journey will be analytical. In the car, on a motorway, you will need to judge when to pull out and when to stay in lane. But you can't afford to be overanalysed. If you do you could cause an accident.

Think about it.

You need the facts, but at some time you need to act.

As already covered in your face will just jump to it without looking at the facts.

Mbti is good at this. However do not take it in its pure form. It is good for a snap shot situation.

You must look at the facts; decide what is of relevance, what information you require, what's not of use yet. You will need a good filing system in your brain and using paper.

Look before you leap.

Best described as:

Mania, Mania, Mania

In the local workingmen's pub two gents (not normally seen here) order beers and sit down. Two local builders are concerned about suited people in their pub.

When one suit goes to the loo, a builder follows him. At the wash basin the builder says "You look smart, what do you do?"

The chap in the suit says, "I am a logical scientist."

The builder says, "What's that?"

The suit says, "I create logical patterns using facts, let's give you a demo."

Builder says "OK"

Suit says, "Do you have goldfish?"

Builder says, "Yes"

Suit says "Pond or bowl?"

Builder says, "Pond, I built it myself"

Suit says, "The fact that you have a pond means you might have a big house"

Builder says" 5 bedrooms, built it myself."

Mania, Mania, Mania

Suit says, "Because you have 5 bedrooms, you might have children."

Builder says " Yes, two lovely kids."

Suit says, " Because you have kids, you have an active sex life."

Builder is looking confused, but still proudly says "Yes."

Suit says, "Finally, you have an active family life, have produced a house to live in, a family life with kids you love and have an active sex live. You are unlikely to masturbate."
Builder says" No way, my sex is on tap."
They leave the loo and go back to their tables.

One suit turns to the other and says "Type 45?"
The other says "Yes, your round."

One builder says to the other "You were there a long time, what did you find out?"

The one that had the demo said, "He is a scientist."

"A what?" he replied.

"Let me give you a demo" he said.

"Ok, do you have goldfish?" he carried on.

The builder looked confused and replied "No"

Mania, Mania, Mania

"You're a wanker," his mate told him, "Your round then, wanker" he carried on.

The facts, the whole facts: that's what you need!!

Think about it.

Actions talk louder than words

The actions of stealth will be more directed than those of in your face.

Mania, Mania, Mania

Judging others

Try not to be too judgemental, because others will judge you.

Hyper maniacs do tend to keep their own council, more so the stealth hyper maniac than the in-your-face.

They know what goes around comes around; they are more likely to force someone to jump than push them.

It's correct that the first impression counts. I was 19 and met a new area manager, some 4 years older than me. My first impression was not good, my old boss had a 2.3litre car he had a 1.6litre car. He dressed badly as if he was in the wrong role and ended up with no respect. At our sales meetings I had no respect for Jim and managed to turn his own team against him. He could not tell the regional manager because he would look like a fool.

It's not only you, it's others, the colour of your clothes is as key as the way you walk and the type of company you are in. For example if you are with a bunch of nerds you will not wear a suit, however bankers always wear pin strip suits.

Some born leaders can wear what they want because they are a born leader. People run them

Mania, Mania, Mania

down because they are jealous rather than not liking what they wear.

And example:
USS Big Ship had her radar down and was heading to port.

"HMS needle to USS Big ship, 12 degrees to port."

"HMS big ship to HMS needle, you move 13 degrees to port."

"HMS needle to USS Big ship, you must move NOW or we will crash."

"USS Big ship to HMS needle, we are the world's biggest aircraft carrier, you move."

"HMS needle to big ship, you move or you will crash, we are a light house."

Think about it.

You will notice that stealth is not really judgemental, unless you really upset them.

While in-your-face does not have a good word to say to anyone.

Mania, Mania, Mania

Leaving a fool

In the kingdom of the blind the one eyed man is the king.

There are plenty of fools around. They will waste your time and send you on wild goose chases. Just steer clear of these fools.

I set up a team once, there where five people in this team and I made sure I knew each person's make up and thinking, how they worked and everything else. They left the company I worked for, to leave for the opposition. I kept in contact with them, they knew my clients, I knew theirs, they ended up stealing each other's clients. I kept mine.

If you have to deal with fools, keep your distance and evolve very little.

I once worked for a company that had a fool; he was the FD. Not because of his qualifications but because his family brought into the business. He gave me a verbal warning for installing software on my PC. I told him that I would not remove it but let the It director remove it. A week after being told off, he came to me because he needed to use this software. Try not to play fools at their own game, you do not need to come down to that level, rather keep your distance.

Mania, Mania, Mania

Think about it.

You will find time when you would not be best putting you head above the shooting line.

In you face just can't do this they can't plat dumb, even if they do not know they will say they do.

While stealth can play dumb, and uses this to their advantage.

Mania, Mania, Mania

Shoot the mentor

Many people have need for a mentor; Anthony Robbins' mentor is a great number of people. The role of the mentor is to help the situation by discussing the issues of the day, in that person's life, give them direction. I have nothing against the few good mentors. I do have an axe to grind for the mentors that destroy hope.

However over the last two years, the cofounder of Chipmunka Publishing has been offered mentoring services. Some of these people should be shot. They are offering high-level solutions where the issue is that someone needs to get the work done. Living in the clouds does not pay the bills.

They like that the consultant will come in with your business situation resolved in their mind. Remember you could (and hyper maniacs are often) better than them. Ask for references first; make sure that they have helped others. Talk to them first on the phone.

I know people that expect results from these people; they need to prove they are good to you. You might need to mentor them. One mentor once offered to change the model of the company that I was involved in: to decrease the amount of admin he recommended putting everything on line via a retailer. I managed to convince the CEO, that this was not best for the business because our GP was

Mania, Mania, Mania

50%. That would reduce it to 20% and out on costs would be the same. The person concerned did not understand the business. One size does not fit all.

To my horror, at a meeting in London, a mentor broker was trying to sell his services. While the candidates do not have experience in our sector, he charged £700 per introduction. We asked for a role and gave a job description; he was unable to fulfil the role.

If you need a mentor (or feel you do) they should be recommended to you and you should feel equal to them.

If you are jack-of-all-trades and master of none, be a mentor.

Think about it.

You see many people wanting to be a mentor, but who mentors the mentor?

In your face will see that the mentor needs to be in the same space as the person they mentor.

In your face will do a great high level mentor, however if things go wrong its the person being mentored that gets the sack, if things are good them then mentor gets the glory.

Mania, Mania, Mania

Shoot the MBA

In the ideal lab, we have control. In the real world it's hell. Most, but not all MBAs live in a sterile world where cause and effect are linear (2D), while life is 3D.

Being an MBA along does not prove anything, being a CEO of a good company and an MBA is different. You only have the MBA, after you have proved yourself.

I admire few MBA's, I admire many people that are making an impact in the world. If Richard Branson studied an MBA would it make him any better? Or if you bought one from the University of South Hampstead.

There are those MBA's that are so good, it's great, and there are those who have had to do it because they can't get a job. I spent sometime with a couple of MBA's and was not impressed, while others I have met I have great regard for.

If you are a poor MBA, you will find the tools area helpful.

If not, do you know:

- How to set up a ltd company in your country on line?

Mania, Mania, Mania

- Where to get audited accounts
- Where to buy websites
- Which type of bank account to have
- How to create money in a business
- Why you take the kitchen sink to all investors meetings
- Why not to use the larger firms
- Do not pay the upfront fee
- Why you do not have to have the property with the business
- When to walk away
- When to roll up your sleeves

If you do not be a constant or mentor, otherwise LEARN from the **tools section**

Think about it.

Your MBA might be very clinical.

The more clinical it is, the more lightly in your face is to have it. He will network well and look good on paper. However not apply what has been taught, as he has not learnt it!

The more practical the MBA the more likely that the stealth has been on the course.

Mania, Mania, Mania

Please note the environment and macroeconomics change too frequently now. If you are on the wrong course then you have been taught the wrong way.
On a personal note, there are no courses that the author can recommend.

Why? Because unless you had your eyes open, the money meltdown of 8.8.2007 could not be foretold. Thereafter the cash injection by the Federal Reserve, ECB and others was not on any lecture.

The last time this was seen was 11.9.2001, nearly five years to the day before.

MBAs, keep your eyes open.

Mania, Mania, Mania

Shoot the consultant

As the consultants teach the trainees: give a man a fish and you can give him another tomorrow, give a man a net and he does not need you.

A great example is:
In our days awash with consultants this should make many of your smile

The Yuppie and the Shepherd: A Modern Day Parable

A shepherd was herding his flock in a remote pasture, when suddenly a BMW charged towards him in a cloud of dust. The driver, a young man in a Prada suit, Gucci shoes, Dior sunglasses and a D&G tie, leans out the window and asks the shepherd: "If I tell you exactly how many sheep you have in your flock, will you give me one?"

The shepherd looks at the man, obviously a yuppie, then looks at his peacefully grazing flock, spread out over an entire pasture and calmly answers, "Sure --- why not?"

The yuppie parks his car, whips out his Dell laptop, connects it to his AT&T mobile phone and surfs to a NASA page on the internet, where he calls up a GPS satellite navigation system to get an exact fix on his location, which he then feeds to another NASA satellite that scans the area in an ultra-high-

Mania, Mania, Mania

resolution photo.

The young man then opens the digital photo in Adobe Photoshop and exports it to an image processing facility in Hamburg, Germany.
Within seconds, he receives an e-mail on his Palm Pilot that the image has been processed and the data stored. He then accesses a MS-SQL database through an ODBC connected Excel spreadsheet with hundreds of complex formulae.

He uploads all of this data via an e-mail on his Blackberry and, after a few minutes, receives a response. Finally, he prints out a full-colour, 150-page report on his hi-tech, miniaturised HP LaserJet printer, turns to the shepherd and says: "You have exactly 1,586 sheep".

"That's interesting. Well, I guess you want one of my sheep," says the shepherd. He watches the young man select one of the animals and looks on amused as the young man stuffs it into the trunk of his car. As he is ready to drive off, the shepherd says, "Hey, if I can tell you exactly what your business is, will you give me back my animal?"

The young man thinks about it for a second and then says: "Okay, why not?"

"You're a consultant," says the shepherd.

"Wow! That's correct," says the yuppie. "But how did you guess that?"

Mania, Mania, Mania

"No guessing required," answers the shepherd. "You showed up here even though nobody called you --- you want to get paid for an answer I already knew --- to a question I never asked --- and you know nothing about my business. Now give me back my **dog**. The number quoted was based on my uncles flock not mine and you pulled this stunt this morning on him"

The consultant knew nothing, even less what he had in his hand. The report offered was not only incorrect but second hand.

They get **you**, to rely on them; they are more dependant on **you**. But they can't let **you** know, that their fat salaries are from you.

Look at the top 4 accounting firms in the 1990's. The audit of accounts was perhaps 20% of the fees. All capped and to a price, while the constancy was 80% of turn over high margin and easy.

You can't ask for a reference from these people. How could you say, "Tom is a creative chap, we enjoyed giving him £200,000 to tell us we were bust. I then sold my house because the bank told me to."

One company that I have met had a turn over of £35,000,000. They injected £400,000 into the

Mania, Mania, Mania

company from its parents just to keep it going. The bank insisted on a full report, costing the company £40,000. All the bank read was the summary: liquidate.
Most consultants I have met, like meetings or even better, meetings about meetings. They really like meetings about meetings, about something that can't happen, in a hotel in the sun at someone's expenses. Because they are so high levelled, anything they want can't happen.

Some of them are to be trusted, but these are not as obvious as not parking the horse out the front. Make sure that they have a passion for your project, double question everything.

I attended a product launch for consultants on HMS Belfast. I sat back and enjoyed the fun; they could not see anything other than their next assignment. I was lucky to meet a chap call Eric (he had a brain). While the others talked about 4-month contracts I explain mine were decided in the first 30 seconds. If they could not or would not change to save their company, I was out. Over 95% stated that they would stay for the fee, not me, I had standards. But they could not see this.

I pointed out how and why the food was presented the way it was. **Most could not get it, but that's consultants for you.**

Mania, Mania, Mania

Think about it.

You might not be surprised that in-your-face consultants love polit studies.

While stealth loves delivery, because there is a real value.

However, the original study needs to be produced with some in-your- face element, otherwise the scope of the project will be wrong.

Therefore the project will fall apart.

Stealth tend to offer "free" consultancy to those they trust, while in your face offer charging for everything including non-related issues.

Mania, Mania, Mania

What comes first?

I have had three years of pain. I have burnt a heap of cash and have 243 product lines to bring to the UK, with a total turnover of £100m per annum. If I had bought a company in the first place I would not have had the time to find these products.

This in most terms is considered, the front (business) or back office (admin and support). I have come to realise that the front office needs to be equal to the back office, however without effective back office (see six sigma) you could lose money without knowing it.

Good front office, we were trying to save a business. The sales director was a head of target. The company was happy, however they had no product to sell as it was all made in china. Some of it had not been made.

You might be the best sales person in the world but without product you have no income or credibility.

Good back office. A dynamic company burnt £120,000 in marketing material for its oil portraits; they had great pens, marketing material and web site. The ordering system was very high Tec. However their only sales person was the CEO. He was considered by most prospects mad. They did not close any business.

Mania, Mania, Mania

You need to do both; production and admin need to feel equal to each other. Then the company will grow. Imbalance creates a loss in both money and staff.

Again it's all down to balance, if it's your money then you need to spend it wisely. Add 10% for over runs and keep the costs under control.

If you are into production find a salesman you can trust; if you are a salesperson find someone good at production and costs.

There is a real need to have a system in place when you get an order, and a person taking the orders.

You might have the best website, with fully integrated SQL, but if no one uses it then what's the point? While if your site is out of date then your shipment might be going out late or the whole business costing you too much.

You and your business need to evolve, but you need to start somewhere. This is called a **vehicle**. The company used it to start the ball rolling.

Think about it.

Mania, Mania, Mania

Your in-your-face will sell a concept, come back with orders then have issues delivering.

Stealth will get a grip of the market, find an in-your-face to sell the product or service, then work out the finer detail.

It is hard doing it from scratch, and with the internet there is no first mover advantage. Best of bread is a safer option to offer.

Mania, Mania, Mania

Six sigma

Six sigma is a principle used to increase productivity in a controlled fashion. There are comities, however when done properly and focused it can produce great results.

Six sigma sits alongside good management, they will apply some principles but not the whole process.

An example of a company not using six sigma is a flat pack company in Rotherham, UK, with a turnover of £35m. It called in the receivers and upon investigation has had one production mess and one sales mess. The production was fundamental, it produced what it wanted, not what the customer wanted. This led to £1m of stock that was over two years old. The sales mess occurred as it only had three customers, because it did not understand sales. Over the year before it stopped trading 750 ranges were produced; in the last few months it was down to 250. These were not high volumes. The directors took out bank loans and started the factory again. In 2005, one of these customers stopped buying flat pack.

Another example of the six sigma principle is an automotive manufacturer which had 37 nuts and bolts on its car. They had 5 shut downs a year and 5 suppliers. They now use 4 nuts and bolts, one

Mania, Mania, Mania

supplier, with one as backup. They are more productive, with better after sales, and more profitable.

Therefore six sigma is designed to make the operation faster and better. Like anything it must be implemented well.

A great book to learn more from is *The Six Sigma Way*, isbn 0071358064

Think about it.

In-your-face does not understand six sigma. He would say he does, however he could not explain it to save his life.

Stealth uses the personal hybrid version. He adapts this to each situation.

Mania, Mania, Mania

Six sigma plus

Six sigma plus follows on from six sigma, looking upstream and downstream for issues.

An example is this: you might be a manufacturer of tyres. Thinking about your new range, should it be upmarket or downmarket?

If there is a shortage of rubber the prices will increase by 30%, therefore you need to be in the premium market to protect yourself.

If you do not use six sigma do use six sigma plus. It will have a far bigger impact on your market.

Everything is becoming a commodity. German farmers are being made bankrupt by cheap under-priced milk in the shops. You will find, as discussed already, that raw material prices like oil are increased. This increases the prices of the product; decreases your margin.

Tesco in the UK have created product deflation over the last 10 years. Jeans are £4, trainers £5 and electrical products cheaper than anywhere else. The only issue is that these products are unbranded; they are made in the same or similar factories. Rather than dealing with product brokers, Tesco are big enough to deal with the factory direct.

Mania, Mania, Mania

Think about it.

This is they hybrid model, not used by in-your-face.

This involves not only macroeconomics, but geopolitical issues too.

This is very hard to explain.

See fourth party logistics: **The Future of Supply Chain Outsourcing?** *ISBN: 9781846930577 published by Best Global Publishing Ltd.*

Mania, Mania, Mania

Swot

Any business book will teach you about SWOT. Strength, weakness, opportunity and threat.

However you can justify most business decisions using a tainted version of swot. There is no correlation or rating in your swot.

A typical chart looks like this:

S.W.O.T.

STRENGHTS:	WEAKNESSES:
THREATS	OPPORTUNITIES

Mania, Mania, Mania

A good step to this first approach is to S.W.O.T. ourselves:

DON'T PANIC!

It has to be laid out accordingly, please do this on paper be real with yourself:

FILL IT IN, Think about IT

DO IT

UNDERSTAND

Mania, Mania, Mania

STRENGTHS:
• Knowledge & Expertise
• Establishment
• Product Quality
• Product Definition
• Service and Accessories
• Image
• Pricing Policy
• Customer Focus
• Planning

OPPORTUNITIES
• Government Legislation
• Industry Standards
• Monopolies
• Market Niches
• Changes in Customer Attitudes
• Exports
• New Technology

Mania, Mania, Mania

WEAKNESSES
<ul><li>Manpower Resources</li><li>Financial Resources</li><li>Knowledge & Expertise</li><li>Lack of Customer Focus</li><li>Product Orientated</li><li>Pricing Policy</li><li>Image</li><li>Sales/After Sales</li></ul>

THREATS
<ul><li>Government Legislation</li><li>Industry Codes of Conduct</li><li>Barriers to Entry</li><li>Price Wars</li><li>Changes in Customer Attitudes</li><li>Imports</li><li>New Technology</li></ul>

Now do Competitors' S.W.O.T.

Competitor 1

Competitor 2

Competitor 3

Mania, Mania, Mania

What do you and your business have going for you? What does the competition have going for them?

A hyper maniac will challenge each entry, give them a weighing and then apply a formula: S + O − W+T = result. This gives a clear picture if the hyper maniac needs to proceed.

Try it; you will be amazed at the results. Justify your actions by fact rather than emotion. If the cars are the same price, but one has better MPG lower cost of ownership but a Skoda badge, you will go for the nice new Ford.

Your SWOT is overridden by emotion.

Example:

A chap has an arranged marriage: he can choose one of three girls. Mary is a size 8 careful with her money and has own flat. Louise is size 12, good job, flash car and lives at home. Emily is size 20, a lawyer and earns over $1,000,000 a year.

Which does he go for? The one with the big tits (emotion).

Mania, Mania, Mania

Think about it.

You are not going to get in-your-face doing a swot or similar unless he has to.

Swap is based around thinking, that's why most in-your-face jump this section.

Mania, Mania, Mania

Streamlining

Streamlining any business creates and loses jobs, money and futures.

Everything is in cycles; the 2005 objective is to outsource everything. This increases return on investment for your investor. Yes, you might lose control, but it's all the fashion.

There are some companies like Dell, Cisco and others using this process, along with e-commerce lead solutions that become faceless and simple to use. Anyone who has used DHL or UPS, will love the online shipping. You can track the parcel in real time; the cost to the business has been great but the number of calls asking where the packet is and who signed for it reduced.

The business does benefit from this type of transaction, however it all depends on your partners; you need to trust them.

A real example is the automotive industry, they use just in time, streamlining and pen book like this:

The production cycle for a mass-market car is held in the main frame, all suppliers can see this data. Let's say that the car needs alloy wheels and leather seats. These are subcontracted from a

Mania, Mania, Mania

supplier, they know that the green seats are required at 10am and they will be fitted at 11am. The contract they have is one hour before, this means delivery is at 9am. There are financial penalties if they do not get it there on time, but by using these methods, they offer effective production. The auto manufacturer can raise billing for them too.

The margin might not be high but the business is so streamlined that it is great.

Ford and other automotive manufacturers try to reduce costs by 5% a year and they can do this by using common parts.

The easiest way of understanding common parts is in fast food production.

The burger house only has 67 raw products in its bill of materials, 4oz burger, 8oz burger, cheese, sauce, big buns, small buns, burger boxes and salad. There are three sizes of cup and six syrups. However they can produce many different flavours and toppings.

It's not what you have got, it's what you do with it.

The downfall of streamlining can be demarcation. If it's not in the contract I am not doing it. In-house teams will understand the common good, others will refer to the contract. This is the difference in partner!!

Think about it.

You might think it's a good idea, however there is a cost to the business.

Why? Because someone somewhere takes the pain.

The operational side would consolidate into some central operations, resulting in more redundancies and greater skill shortages.

Mania, Mania, Mania

Fiscal 2

Do not believe the accounts. Because you have a clean driving licence does not mean that you have not been stopped for drinking and driving.

The accounts of a company can be 18 months out of date, in the case of Parmalat, Enron and others they could be wrong. While they give you a good snapshot of the company, there are issues that need addressing.

Most companies using the new accounts standards are bust. Many are cash cows, producing cash before it's due on small margins (supermarkets); the balance sheet looks good but the business is not. Others are geared rather too heavily. If a company has millions of assets and the bank won't lend it further funds, does that not say something?

Read the bluffers' guide to accounting, this will get you on the right track. The accountants are there for a role; it's not in your interest to find out what that role is.

The new accounting standards will make it clearer who has no money and who to invest in. But watch out for things off the books ...

Mania, Mania, Mania

Think about it.

You might not think it but the facts tell a trend. This trend might be more cash (cash cow) or less cash, (bad management).

Three years audit account can't hide the facts, even if you are Enron. From here you mark a trend of where the business is going.

Look at changes in product line, directors and market place.

For companies it is hard to raise money without bank support.

Fiscal 2 is only one tool, not the only tool in the toolbox.

Mania, Mania, Mania

Understanding your limitations

Inspirational quote
Know your enemy and know yourself
Sun Tzu, The Art of War

If you can't do it, you can't. You might want to learn.

I recently had to move a site to PHP for a company. While I understand HTML, Java and JavaScript I know nothing about SQL and PHP.

I did something wrong and told the IT chap, I do not know what I am doing, I can't fly a plane, do brain surgery or repair an engine. If I do it wrong again it's because I do not know what I am doing.

There are some things you just can't do, there are others where you learn to do them. There are yet more where you just do not want to do them.

Before PCs were mainstream, I worked for a company who every day had to interface with the mainframe computer. After 4 weeks I ended up doing it but I did not enjoy it. So I did it wrong one day and was banned by the boss from doing it. Everyone but him knew that I wanted to move on and I did.

Mania, Mania, Mania

There are times when you need not get your hands dirty, just move on to the bigger picture, while there are other times when you need to prove you can do it. There might be times when you want to see how others could do it.

Know your limitations and stick to what you know. Hypo maniacs tend to spoil things that they do not know.

Think about it.

You will not see an in-your-face restraining himself. They prefer to get knocked down, and then just say they do not know.

In-your-face might try, but will not bluff it or lie.

Mania, Mania, Mania

Boo.com

Do read the book, you will see a company who had it all, yet had nothing.

There are businesses I have invested in that have been before or after the crest of the wave. You must consider this opportunity and if it will do what is says on the tin.

By offering a better product for less money or more effective solutions is that going to in?

Boo.com had the back end sorted at a cost, but the front end just was not there. They had investors to worry about. They needed money like it was going out of fashion.

The final resolve was not the best. Just be careful, others judge you by your failure, it's better not to back a horse than to back a loser.

There are many examples of markets moving to keep the investor out. The stock market is the ideal one as it goes up and down. For some periods it might trade sideways.

People in the UK were piling into buy-to-let after the party had finished. Do your own homework; you will win more than you lose.

Mania, Mania, Mania

You fail your first five businesses to succeed in others.
Think about it.

Boo.com is a telling story to get you thinking about how having just a page on the Internet would sell your product.

However this is not true.

Mania, Mania, Mania

Learning to walk away

This is a continuation of the previous subject. If it is not for you, walk away.

They might be fair, or only ask for £10,000, but after doing your homework if it does not add up walk away.

I have already told you about the job that was wrong. But there are not only jobs but also companies.

Would you buy a house if it was valued at £300,000 with a monthly repayment of £1500 and rental income of £2000? That's what they told you, but the difference between perception and reality kick in: the small print said that this rental was for 6 months; thereafter it was at the market rate (£600). What would you do now?

Yes, I have bought houses and land without seeing it, but I did my homework.

Often you can't even talk to the people, just distance yourself from them, that's all you can do.

Mania, Mania, Mania

<u>Think about it.</u>

You can't get on with the situation so walk away. In-your-face would only walk away if they where either being undermined or found out.

Mania, Mania, Mania

The 80/20 rule

This maintains that 80% of effort produces 20% of the result. And it does.

You might have a client list: on which the ones which need to have their hands held are taking up your time and only producing 20% results. The ones who come in and out are the ones you need.

By focusing on who creates more margins, not turnover for you or your business, you can create more value. Increased value means increased worth.

Increased turnover could lead to increased work and very little return.

Reduce your interaction with time-wasters, think smart.

Think about it.

80% of the time in-your-face can force the issue, 20% of the time you can break him with the facts.

Mania, Mania, Mania

Winning

You are a winner; you will win:

Whatever the battle you aim to win. The methods have partly been discussed in the sections on Genghis Khan and Sun Tzu.

No matter what you do aim to win, an easier way of doing this is have good team players. While they might not get on with each other in times of trouble, they can cover each other.

Winning is to think of what you do in everyday life; just by taking part you might be winning. Each day has its battle, win the battle and win the war.

You are a winner; you will win.

Think about it.

You are a winner, whichever type you are. I think therefore I am.

Mania, Mania, Mania

Playing the fool

The fool or patsy should be avoided; you do not want to be like them. However sometimes you have to play the fool.

Once on a business trip I was in the company of an in-your-face sales person. He was not a hyper maniac, just a salesman. I was to present to an overseas lender so I needed him on my side. Therefore I played the fool to him and I waited for every word (or so he thought), I was the lap dog. However I needed this contract, I needed the funds for my project but I also needed to know how this chap worked.

We spent 4 days together and I just let him talk. While I could not take him head on, I could start to question some of his statements.

By day two, I had what I came for, the offer on funding. Therefore I needed to work on this chap. The more I questioned, the more he gave out and guess what, 80% were lies. At a debrief to a team member, who was keen to offer his projects to the lender, I proved that what had been told in the UK was not true and could not be done. All of the information extracted from the chap was used as proof.

Mania, Mania, Mania

Fools are easy to spot. Look at the news, there is someone reading a statement, they do not know the situation, they are just there to present the statement. The people behind the action want to stay out of the firing line.

Keep your friends close, but your enemies closer still.

Think about it.

You might have to play dumb, but not if you're in-your-face!

Mania, Mania, Mania

The truth about money

Money is useful, however the love of money is the root of all evil.

Money is also a state of mind; *Think And Grow Rich* is a good book.

This is true. As greed takes over, there are people left behind. I am not saying you should sell all you have, but rather be careful with money. You will need to borrow it and pay it back.

Since the enterprise act of September 2004, people and companies in the UK have become more flexible in their understanding of money. However banks and lenders do not like risk. The bad debt (not performing loans) in Japan is so vast that the numbers are scary.

Just by playing a simple game of monopoly you can find out how people are with money. Do you buy no houses and the money runs out towards the tail end of the game? Do you buy all the property that you land on and become asset rich cash poor? Or are you in the middle?

It's very easy to spend money, much harder to save it.

Mania, Mania, Mania

Think about it.

In-your-face as shown spends money, not caring if it's his or someone else's.

See quote from the late George Best 'I have spent a lot of money on drink, drugs and women. I squandered the rest'.

In-your-face is more selective about his investments.

Mania, Mania, Mania

Sun tzu

The Art of War is such an inspiration. However it was designed to be a practical in life and war.

However most people use this book as a coffee table book or to add to their CV as last book read.

It is a practical book. My son who plays Rome Total War is reading it (aged 12), not for a good read but for a good battle.

Why do people buy presents like cookbooks? Because the receiver is crap at cooking? Why do people buy their contacts many gifts? To highlight in a non-verbal way where they need to improve.

Sun Tzu covers battles - while the principles are similar, he covers battles. Sandhurst and other army training centres are still using the theory. But furthermore they are applying the principle.

Why have a book in French if you have not read it or the complete collection of Shakespeare still in the box?

We are here to live and learn, hence the author only reads in a focused fashion.

Mania, Mania, Mania

Think about it.

You need to read about the ways of war, because life is a war with both good and evil changing everyday.

Mania, Mania, Mania

Genghis Khan

What a man. He concluded internal conflict before resolving external conflict.

Yes, he did kill many of his own countrymen, but it was kill or be killed. He had a system that worked, he would offer peace and if not taken, there would be bloodshed. The stories of his tribe doing everything on their horses are true. To bring the tribe into line, he would kill those that did not stand with him, leaving only those under two feet to be added to the extended tribe. Once he was king, he picked out other countries but he used stealth.

He would go to a border town, seek peace (or occupation). If they did not agree he would kill them all, except the scribes. They would be set free to tell the next town what was coming (viral marketing). He would use the towns' own animals to stamp the towns, he would use people in cities.

He adapted and became better, understood trade between conquering cultures. He would use daring to attack forces. He would promote people that had skills. They need not be from his tribe, he could trust them.

What has this got to do with businesses?

Mania, Mania, Mania

He forced the competition out of the market. Shut off supplies, created fear, viral marketing, free trade and learnt how other people work.

Think about it.

You have heard that he killed people, however those that he trusted were part of the team too.

He used each situation to defeat the enemy.

Mania, Mania, Mania

Why do they do it?

Why do people in power spoil everything?

The real reason is that they think that they are above the law. Taking money from the shareholders or pension fund (Robert Maxwell).

Spending $2m on the CEO's wife's birthday party (TYCO).

They hide things from the accountant (Pamalat) or hide things with the help of accountants.

They think no one can touch them, yet they do.

They do it, but one day get found out. When they get found out the house of cards comes down. Much like a kiss from a pretty girl, it's nice, but stay around for too long and you will suffer.

They do it YOU MUST NOT DO IT.

Think about it.

You know in-your-face, meet them, see them on TV. Why do they do it?

Mania, Mania, Mania

Reality check

You need to make sure you are on the ground rather than in the air.

Do you know how much the cost of milk is or a loaf of bread? There are people who earn a great deal of money who do not. I worked with a chap call Vic Kithener: a great man, but had no sense of reality. Before I met him he was very high up in Wang, earning £20,000 per month in 1990. He had people to do everything, clean, drive etc. and his kitchen was spotless because he always ate out.

He was good with money but had no sense of reality. The same happens in business: doing a business plan is easy. Doing one that stacks up is even easier (I had done plenty). However, doing one that reflects both the business and reality is hard.

You have to be honest, if you are not then it's not the lender you are fooling, it's YOU. You see, if you budget for losses that's OK, but if you budget for increased profits that do not turn up then that's bad.

Look at companies for sale, they say put the owners' salary back in the business. You could but how many extra staff at what cost should you budget for? How key is the owner?

Mania, Mania, Mania

You have read about perception and reality. Well, it needs to be real for people to buy into it. Or it's just a concept that goes nowhere.

Think about it.

Your challenge is to think about your life and do something with it; you are considering this because you have read this book.

Mania, Mania, Mania

The truth about the internet

The internet was designed during the cold war to be used as a communication tool. Much of this has been documented.

It has evolved into an information and disinformation tool. There are many scams on the net and as we are going to describe in viral marketing you can find out a great deal from the Internet.

The Internet is a double-edged sword, you need to offer the same product to all on the Internet otherwise they will find out. Some retailers offer cheaper products on the net. This is because they have lower costs for this type of transaction.

The customer can find out a great deal about your product ranges and therefore THEY decide when to buy. If you look at the PC market - promise your children a PC for Christmas but buy it in the new year saving 10% - of if you know Intel are bringing out a new chip buy it 4 weeks after this faster chip comes out. Because the older chips drop in price.

The internet can also change the way you interface in business. You can have a full report on the company or person within five minutes. You might still be talking to them on the phone.

Mania, Mania, Mania

You might be given a medical product, great, you can find out its side effects on the Internet.

The only personal issue is that the Internet is changing the way we communicate with each other. There is less done face to face and more in written form. This does not allow interaction.

Product demand can change like the wind, good and bad information can be found at the drop of a hat.

Think about it.

You must see the Internet as a tool.

Tools can be used for both good and bad, you have the tool in your hand, are you going to send an e-mail for war or peace?

Mania, Mania, Mania

Viral marketing

Where to begin? Think of viral marketing as a virus!!!!

It's a circle before 1500 AD 99% of history was folklore, people around campfires telling tales.

Around 100 BC there was localised writing, people documenting facts and people, a sort of historic record.

Before the Industrial Revolution the upper classes wrote letters, postcards etc. although the middle class or working class could not always read or write.

Post Industrial Revolution, newspapers could be produced and more people were reading.

After 2000 the Internet became a tool.

You have five stages: let's look at them more closely in detail.

Media moved from one to one, to educated masses, to all masses, to one to one.

We sold our own vegetables, we sold our product to those who can read, we sold our product in supermarkets to the masses and we sold it on the net as an exclusive organic product.

Mania, Mania, Mania

The adoption of technology has increased. It took 10 years for the train to go from the UK to America, seven years for VHS to take off, 3 years for DVD to reach the masses and 18 months for MP3.

We adopt technology now without knowing your new mobile will have double the features of the last at a lower price. Manufacturers and producers want you to consume and they add features to help this happen, however the reality is that their profits are in decline, not increasing.

Viral marketing in effect takes us to where we started, in the global market we sell one to one. If you need facts on a product to purchase it, you look on the net.

Time to market is weeks and not years, you can produce in smaller volumes.

The product shift can take 4 hours rather than weeks or months. If a drug has bad press then people stop using it the same day. MMR vaccination is a good example. It had bad press in 2005 in the UK. And the number of children having it fell. This in turn created an issue with the doctors and the impedance is still waiting to happen.

You have 4 billion potential customers who, if they buy might buy direct or via your distribution channels. You have to have enough products to

Mania, Mania, Mania

keep them happy but not enough to make the bank cry.

If people find a product cheaper in another country the will buy it there. I saved 23% on a new car buying it on the Internet.

Viral marketing helped *hotmail.com* come onto the market and get into the top 5 in a very short period of time. Its power cannot be underestimated.

You can do viral marketing and you do. Every one person who is unhappy about a product will tell 12 other people. It's a fact, what do you think of estate agents or banks?

I rest my case.

Think about it.

You understand people buy from people. Marketing of this kind requires people to talk about something; it could be Google or You Tube, or the bad government of a country.

Mania, Mania, Mania

There will always be an England

The role of England has always been unique. For example, while in Queen Victoria's day the sun did not set on the empire, England still has a few ticks left.

When Margaret Thatcher was voted out of the party in 1984, there were many countries that wanted her and her reforms. Those reforms are challenging the very strong powerhouses of Europe, France and Germany. These countries are stuck in a mire of unemployment, bad working practices and heavy national debt.

Every nation will have its day. In biblical times it was Ethiopia, Egypt, Greece, then Rome (or Italy) then Genghis Khan and his hoard. The Industrial Revolution happened in the UK, and the UK was an invader until after the Second World War. Germany tried to take over (twice).

While the UK is not liked throughout Europe, it still has a financial role to play in banking. The currency is fundamentally sound. However labour costs are high, employment is low. London is the most expensive capital in Europe for many things.

The recent bombing of London proved that there is a stiff upper lip; the people killed were not Caucasian (white) suited and booted people but

Mania, Mania, Mania

rather normal mixed race people. England is not full of white faces, but rather is a mixed race culture.

My local Church of England school has 210 pupils, and 26 of these do not have English as their first language. You might think this is a bad school? Well, the boys do better than the girls. Why? They want to be like their fathers, who are accountants, doctors and professionals: they have a dream.

This school is not on its own; however there are others that have similar composition. They are full of the same colour and have NO dreams, NO expectations and NO life.

You have got to have a dream, how otherwise can you have a dream come true?

Think about it.

You might not know it but on 8 August 2007 the UK government was one of the only G8 countries not to put money into the economy.

Be supportive to your country, or move to one you can support.

Mania, Mania, Mania

They came from the East

In May 2004, 10 countries were allowed into the European Union. While NATO was happy, this changed the balance of power and landscape of the EU.

The original club of 12 were comfortable, however the large group had so many issues to address it's no wonder the French voted no.

The old club had the tiger economy of Ireland and Greek issues, along with the two powerhouses, France and Germany. The EU created a currency that would help the common good and when it did other countries wanted some of that action.

These countries will be the new tiger economies. They have a cheap and willing workforce with a politically stable constitution, while the average salary for Germany is €38,000, France €30,000 and Spain €18,000. These countries are up to 50% unemployed, with more flexible labour and an average salary of €5,000.

They needed to join because they had always been part of a group, however they have similar issues to the old EU. The tiger economies are Lithuania, Poland and the Czech Republic. Like some of the other countries, these countries had fundamental issues to address. They have only been used to

Mania, Mania, Mania

capitalism for 12 years and are still trying to cope with unemployment, redundancy and similar problems. They are all proud people and even the unemployed clean the street.

A national paper owner at an embassy party put it like this. Under Communism we had money but no goods and under Capitalism we have goods but no money. Many of these countries have had things they did not have for the last 50 years; they have reached their dreams.

However, some factories are being moved from these countries to China, as the wages are too high.

The 20 – 35 age group are highly educated and ready to work, however they are often unable to find work. All of these countries have been force to find flexible working conditions.

They are going to be the new powerhouse of Europe.

Think about it.

The population of Europe needs employment; otherwise the economy will go down the drain. Therefore we also need to support Europe, until the next separation of countries.

Mania, Mania, Mania

Where is China?

At the time of writing China had still pegged its currency to the Dollar. Alan Greenspan had just delivered a talk in New York. There is pressure from the US to unpeg and devalue. The effect of this on the US economy is too much. The price of goods could rise by 20%, this giving inflation to the US economy. The producers would look to other Asian countries for cheap manufactured product.

China is known to be issuing 50% more RMB instruments that it should, but what Greenspan could not say was since these are pegged to the Dollar they are in effect building a Dollar reserve. This is worse for the US as 40% of all the bonds are held by China and Japan. They need these countries to buy at least $78T in 2006.

China needs to be known, they have transformed their country from subsistence to manufacturing. However the pain of growth is great, they are currently a net importer of raw material. They soon will be an exporter. In the case of steel, for example, they will move in 2007 from importer to exporter. Just watch the price fall.

On a human level, 30 years ago you would be asked when did you last eat? 10 years ago rice was the staple food, meat like chicken only eaten on holy days. However now you have 1.4 billion people, all looking to eat every day. The average

Mania, Mania, Mania

wage is a Dollar a day and two bowls of rice. However the consumer economy is so large everyone wants some of it.

Currently, there is not enough electricity for the country. The 6 regions are taking it in turns to go without it. This increase the amount of fuel purchased and has a knock-on effect on the economy.

Shanghai province will soon challenge that of California. This will prove difficult for some governments to come to terms with.

Think about it.

China is a sleeping power, along with India; there is a large population in each.

There is a growing middle class in these countries. This middle class would spend a great deal of money, helping both the economy for the country and the global economy.

Mania, Mania, Mania

What hope the world?

It's your world, you made the mess, please can you tidy it up?

There is war, famine, pollution and corruption. These things are all over the world. There are the natural resources that are being used up like there is no tomorrow. Greed and fear (as already shown) are used to control the masses.

At the tender age of 16 I saw parts of the Far East before they started ripping it apart. You have been given this mess; will you give a bigger issue to the next generation?

Single people occupy 40% of homes in the UK and while life expectancy increases, the need to consume everything, including each other, is worse than it ever was.

There is starting to be a shift of power, China might have the power that Japan dreamt of? Or will the USA still keep control of 1.4 billon people?

Not controlling carbon emissions might increase profit and kill customers; not treating water might sound fun but could kill your workers. Look at the Rhine, it starts crystal clear in the Swiss Alps and after passing three countries it goes into the sea. Almost every mile they take some water out and put it back in a worst state. The people need this water to drink, for farming, for industry. But they are without doubt polluting it.

You have the power of one (covered earlier) therefore your vote counts. The difference that you can make is so vast. It might be adopting a child or the giving of aid but in 100 years, unless we are in space, this point is going to be unliveable for another 400 million years.

Think about it.

The pace of the world is changing. You can see the pace of technology:

VCR: 10 years
DVD: 5 years
MP3: 2 years

If it's good you can see a market for your product.

If there is a disaster then the whole world needs to know and they can.

Mania, Mania, Mania

Europe, the bigger picture

Europe for many has moved from the Common Market to a group of 25 countries that all need each other to fight against (in trade terms) other groups.

Countries outside the current Euro zone want to get in, while countries that are in want to get out. There is too much in fighting and the need to solve the common issues is often left behind.

You can operate in most of the countries but you will find that some countries will be cheaper and tax-free. You must consider that there is no common language among the countries. They are like the USA with no common tax. In mainland Europe people and businesses do migrate to suit their needs.

Comply with the basic requirement, you might have to have 25 serviced offices (they hate ringing outside their own country), you will need staff that can really talk the same LOCAL language and you need to solve those very nasty distribution problems. While the banking system is great, the fundamentals need addressing.

Germany and France, the powerhouses of Europe, are not prosperous at the moment, due partly to strict labour laws. Once they are up and running, the European economy should be better off. However, they have unemployment of 10%

Mania, Mania, Mania

compared to less than 5% in the UK and Ireland. It will take some time before they can regain control.

The countries are not polarised into one extra, they are both extremes. They have though a common need.

I do not think that Europe can last in its current state, the no vote will see to that. The need is for reform but how this is now done is for others to decide.

The same is true of Europe as with the USA, find a friendly state and start there. The currency should be stable.

Think about it.

Europe is a powerhouse: French finance ministers are cutting out the red tape, Germany has a woman prime minister.

If the economy was in good shape then Europe could challenge others, however Europe keeps on going, taking in new countries, one day Turkey will be part of the EU too.

Mania, Mania, Mania

USA and the inside track

The USA is a great market, however it is governed by 50 plus different sets of laws. Only 20% of the population have passports. You must budget to get into this market then double the amount you expect to spend. As the amount of litigation is vast; you must have good cover on your service or product. If you are not covered you could lose it all.

This is a do-or-die country. Do it and you will have an income, don't and you could die. Fashion can change in days and it varies from state to state. To enter the US market or to stay in it you need to constantly reinvent yourself. If you do not have deep pockets, or the desire to tame the US market, then just sell your product to this market on the internet.

They are great people and a few percentage points of the total market will make you big bucks. However, the cost of going into this market might be too big. There are many products to sell, but you are better involving your customers in this market or even buying an existing business rather than going into it.

They are the easiest market to approach; you have over 360 million people understanding a common tongue. You, as always, need to start in one state. Choose the easiest for your product, then work outwards.

Mania, Mania, Mania

The international policies are great, as are the needs of the people; the trend is to better fuel-efficient cars and modes of transports. There is also a great divide between rich and poor. The demand for consumer goods is great and although they have great natural resources themselves, they buy in a high volume of overseas product.

Think about it.

America is a great, however there are many global microcosmical issues.
Like many G8 countries it would help if they could reduce the national debt
If we knew what worked we would not waste our money on the rest.

There are different ways of selling; you must understand your customer, whether B2C or B2B social group, their buying patterns and what they like to buy.

As discussed, in viral marketing we are focusing on an individual purchase. Tesco have poured millions into their club card - they have the software to identify what an individual customer buys. This is the type of data we are taking about. Everything comes in cycles, just like the seasons of the year. Fashions keep on coming back, and there is always a different form of new media. With marketing you

Mania, Mania, Mania

need to decide whether it's better to do none than do the wrong form of marketing.

You could hire an expensive team that are crap, or do it yourself more effectively. The tool section of the book should help you. If you get a consultant in, then ask for two hours free, then a written brief. Take this brief and do as much of it as you can.

The best long-term marketing campaign was also the worst. New Coke was for the new generation, it cost the company $100m, but the profile raised the brand. No one liked it, but the customer (to whom you market) demanded old coke back. They had interaction with the customer; this is what you need in marketing.

You can't market safe sex to the over 80s, or bed pants to the under 25s. Be careful of your marketing, careful that you are targeting the correct people. You might find that referrals work far better than marketing.

It is better to send out nothing than send out rubbish, as the person getting your marketing material will have a dim view of you.

Be careful not be the first or the last to sell to a particular market. If you are the first to try a new marketing campaign, the agency will use you to learn how to do it, if you are the last then the market will be saturated.

Mania, Mania, Mania

You could be marketing yourself, but are you marketable?

Think about it.

Mania does make you marketable.

Mania, Mania, Mania

Meetings

Be a man of action. What is the purpose of the meeting?

We have already discussed consultants and meetings - try and stay out of these. If you do go, opt in for the jobs you can do effectively. Where the meeting is high-level and you know the grassroots stuff, then all you need to do is be present: you can do this effectively.

I once did some constancy, for a £35m manufacturer of good standing. They would ring up every other week saying that they had urgent news. Once when I had travelled 150 miles I found out it was only to have a chat.

I arranged a sales call (but called it a satisfaction meeting) with a big broker; not only did I leave with many orders every day of this week but also got to know his production schedule.

Unproductive meetings waste time, and time is not something you can have back. Ask to see the agenda for the meeting. If there is not an agenda submit your own, if they do not accept it then you might refuse to go.

Control the meeting, directly or indirectly, if you do not agree then "pass", if you do not understand, ask them to explain.

Mania, Mania, Mania

By not being invited to meetings you are not in the loop, where you are in the meeting take your own notes, as the minutes might not be a true reflection on the meeting. I once worked in a company where the CEO took delight in adjusting the minutes of a sales meeting to reflect his greatness.

Where you have no faith in the chair of the meeting or the direction you or the other attendees will talk over the chairman's direction or even just not turn up.

At one company I worked for we had a bacon sandwich at the meeting: this soon lost its appeal after 7 meetings. Do not go unless you can contribute something of value or you need to know something about the subject.

By being informed and directing the discussion you do not need not take up the chair role to steer the meeting but rather you can keep things going because of what you know.

Think about it.

Do you want to attend meaningless meetings?

Mania, Mania, Mania

Do one well or 90 badly?

Would you prefer to do one job well? Or 90 badly?

This is the issue in today's environment, it's easy to do 90 jobs but to do one well is better. You can't afford to be Jack-of-all-trades but master of none. You can learn new skills but you will find that once you have one skill the others will be easy to do.

As you learn ONE skill you will be a true master, as you progress to learning something different many of the skills will be similar. A child only learns to walk once or write once. When moving to a country where a different language is spoken often the letters are the same, it's only the meaning that has changed.
If you can't read or write in your native tongue what hope have you got with this new language?

When going to an interview they might ask for strengths and weaknesses. You are better off having good employable strengths than a heap of weaknesses.
Play to your strengths and get others to cover your weaknesses, you will find if you are a hyper maniac then you WILL be strong.

Mania, Mania, Mania

Think about it.

Do one thing well. Only in-your-face has 99 things on the go, and all of these badly.

Hyper mania what now?

Welcome to the point that starts making sense.

Your life is just that: your life.

You need to take control of it; there are plenty of people out there to help.

Have your trusted contacts and that's it, no more, just them.

Read the other books and live life to the full.

Think about it.

Control your mania....

Mania, Mania, Mania

Profile worker

Your life as a hyper manic will be a constant move from job to job, from one thing to the next.

You will find however that you start to build up a bank of contacts if you keep in touch. Often these people will want to keep in touch with you to find out what is going on. For the hypo manic, life can be full of extremes. You will be chasing old contacts that you have neglected, while the bank could be chasing you.

THINK TWICE THEN ACT!

Think about it.

There are no jobs for life, however in-your-face might change jobs more frequently than you think, every year, or even every week.

Mania, Mania, Mania

Reality check

You need to do this yourself; find someone you can trust to talk about it.

Sorry if you are a hypo maniac, just go for it. The answers were in the book. Have fun.

Think about it.

Do think about your life, as you only have one.

Mania, Mania, Mania

That action plan

Your need is to plan, don't just leave work.

Plan, think about what you do and what you like, then go and do it.

Mania is great such a high, without drugs.

Revisit your action plan every week and think about what you need to learn.

Save money, but above everything, enjoy LIFE.

Think about it.

Plan for greatness not failure.

Mania, Mania, Mania

Coming to terms with Mania

Your life might make more sense now.

The fact of you leaving all that disaster behind you or the wondering what life is about will help.

Come to terms with it, don't fear it. Embrace it, for your purpose it has been revealed.

These so-real dreams that you can't forget, do not let them worry you but look forward to them.

Sure you might get low, but you are probably the best salesman in the company.

Now you begin to understand, go get that tiger.

Think about it.

The sooner you come to terms with mania the better.

Mania, Mania, Mania

I need help!!

Your life might start to make sense now.

You will start to control more of your everyday experience, what you do and how you do it.

Once you decide to change, the rest is easy.

Help needed? No, understanding and love.

Think about it.

Talk about it to people you trust.

Mania, Mania, Mania

Read

Hyper Mania Explained

Packed with expert advice, this book will help you cope with your own hyper mania or help someone else with the problem.

This is a difficult problem and there is a further book on the subject.

Do you get it yet?

Gives a blow-by-blow account of mania. This pulls no punches and takes no prisoners. This book has been written by an ex hyper maniac and a bipolar. These people set up Chipmunka to help save the world. It might just open your eyes or the eyes of your loved one.

Both published by Chipmunka Publishing

Mania, Mania, Mania

Think about it.

You only get one life, treat it with respect.

Mania, Mania, Mania

Why do they do it?

Why do people in power spoil everything?

The real reason is that they think that they are above the law. Taking money from the shareholders or pension fund (Robert Maxwell).

Spending $2m on the CEO's wife's birthday party (TYCO).

They hide things from accountant (Pamalat) or hide things with the help of accountants.

They think no one can touch them, yet they do.

They do it but one day get found out. When they get found out the house of cards comes down. Much like a kiss from a pretty girl, it's nice but stay around for too long and you will suffer.

They do it YOU MUST NOT DO IT

Think about it.

You are responsible for your actions, not other people.

Mania, Mania, Mania

Postscript

Understand your life or be a bystander: the choice is yours……..

You are loved
You are special
You are you
You need direction
You need faith
You can do it
You are the only thing holding you back every day

You have Power, Love and Self-Control: Hyper maniac

You have power: Hypo maniac

Hypo maniac learn,
Be stronger
Understand
And then have love
For as Rome was not built in a day you need patience.

Mania, Mania, Mania

www.ingramcontent.com/pod-product-compliance
Ingram Content Group UK Ltd.
Pitfield, Milton Keynes, MK11 3LW, UK
UKHW041410180426
11947UKWH00007B/43